Spinner Fishing
For Steelhead,
Salmon and Trout

Third Edition

Jed Davis

©1985 H. ROOKS

Frank Amato Publications • P.O. Box 82112, Portland, Oregon 97282 • (503) 653-8108

Frank Amato Publications, P.O. Box 82112, Portland, Oregon 97282

Cover design and inside illustrations: Howard Rooks
Cover photo: Robert M. Pearlman — Book design: Joyce Herbst

©1985, Second Edition 1989, by Jed Davis
Published 1985. Second Edition 1989. Third Edition 1995
Printed in Hong Kong

Library of Congress Cataloging in Publication Data

Davis, Jed.
    Spinner Fishing for Steelhead, Salmon, and Trout / Jed Davis. —
3rd ed.
        p.   cm.
    Includes indexes.
ISBN 0-936608-40-4 (pbk.) : $19.95

1. Spin-fishing.   2. Steelhead fishing.   3. Salmon-fishing.
4. Trout fishing.   I. Title
SH456.5.D38   1989
799.1'755--dc19   88–31377
                                                       CIP

INTRODUCTION

When Frank Amato and I discussed my idea, *Spinner Fishing for Steelhead, Salmon and Trout* back in 1983, we had no idea that it would become a best-selling book. Spinner fishing for steelhead is a very specialized topic. But also, one must remember that in 1982, the year I began writing this book, serious spinner fishing for steelhead was virtually nonexistent in the Pacific Northwest and practiced by relatively few anglers in the Great Lakes. How things have changed! Spinner fishing for steelhead is now commonplace. What's more, it is the fastest growing steelhead technique nationwide, attracting novices as well as converts from more traditional methods.

I see any fishing technique as being in a constant state of development and refinement. Thus, when comparing this third edition to the previous editions, changes have been made that are a reflection of greater experience, awareness and the further development of technique and tackle. So if you are one of the many anglers who wrote to me and said that you read the book six times (I'm still trying to figure this one out), you will notice a few minor changes with regard to technique. However, the basic framework remains unchanged. In fact, I am probably more confident of my theories and techniques than when I originally wrote about them. This is largely due to the positive feedback I have received from literally thousands of anglers.

If there is one major change to this edition, it would have to center around my understanding, development and refinement of spinners and components. Ever since 1982, I have been experimenting with ways of improving spinner designs and spinner components. After years of using some of the compo-nents featured on the color plate of the older editions of this book, I became excited about the possibility of designing spinners and components that would be geared to the specific needs of steelhead and salmon anglers. I therefore started to develop and manufacture my own components with the idea of opening up a mail-order division through Pen Tac Corporation, a tackle manufacturing firm I started in the early 1980s. I have deleted the old products and now feature the new Pen Tac products on the color plate and in Chapter 14 since these were designed specifically for the uses outlined in this book.

Spinner fishing for steelhead is a marvelous sport. There is nothing quite like the powerful jolt of a mint-bright winter-run or the hysterical charge of a summer-run in 18 inches of gin-clear water. The spinner's ability to infuriate, excite and pro-voke allows us to see these marvelous gamefish in ways that could never be experienced with other methods. And that, along with effectiveness, is why this exciting technique is gaining so rapidly in popularity.

The publishing of this book has meant a lot to me and my greatest satisfaction has come from having made a contribution to a sport that I worship. Every time I receive a letter from an angler who had success with these techniques, I feel a wonderful sense of fulfillment. Therefore, this edition of *Spinner Fishing for Steelhead, Salmon and Trout* is dedicated to those anglers who made this third edition possible.

Jed Davis
October 19, 1993

Acknowledgements

I would like to thank the following individuals for their contributions and support.

Cindy Routtu for a fine typing and editing job; Howard Rooks for his superb graphic talent; Asa Pearl for his excellent slide-taking under adverse conditions; Frank Amato for his confidence in me; my father, David Davis, for introducing me to the sport that became my profession; and my wife Lori who is everything I ever hoped for in a life partner.

About the Author

Jed Davis has been an avid steelheader since the 1960s, a time when the Great Lakes were rejuvenated with coho, Chinook, and steelhead. His career as an outdoor writer began while completing his doctoral work at the University of Michigan (Ph.D. 1980). In 1981, he moved, with his wife Lori, from Ann Arbor, Michigan to Eugene, Oregon where he pioneered spinner fishing techniques for taking McKenzie steelhead as well as helping to popularize what he quickly recognized as one of the great unknown steelhead fisheries in North America.

Now living in Bellevue, Washington, he is a regular contributor to *Salmon Trout Steelheader*, and also writes for *Trout, Western Outdoors*, and several other publications. His firm, Pen Tac Corporation, in Woodinville, Washington, is the world's only supplier of spinners and components that relies totally on in-house manufacture. His company also supplies components and custom automated machinery to other tackle manufacturers around the world.

In addition to his fishing interests, he has twin daughters and a son. He plays basketball in city leagues, is an L.A. Laker fanatic, a shortwave radio buff, and of course a dedicated river, lake, and Puget Sound angler. His current special interest is the history of fast-food architecture.

FISHING ROOTS

MY FISHING ROOTS GO BACK AT LEAST 500 years to a time when Eastern European Jewry was a dominant culture in Poland, Romania, Hungary and Russia. My grandmother, now 85, tells of the small unspoiled streams that trickled down from the Carpathian Mountains surrounding her native Rona de Jos, a sleepy village in the northern Maramures Province of Romania. Like generations before her, she would walk through the woods every Friday morning to a large pool where she knew there would be good numbers of fish. Then, she would take out the mysterious herb called *mazlak* ("maz" as in Mazda and "lak" as in locksmith) which grew naturally on poppies that were indigenous to the region. The dried out poppy seeds would be ground and then imbedded in small pieces of liver. The fish, probably brown trout, would snap up the liver and then, once dazed, would slowly move to the surface, still swimming upright. My grandmother would then take what she needed for sweet and sour fish, a traditional Jewish delicacy served as an appetizer on the eve of the Jewish Sabbath. As for the other dazed trout, they were left to work off their hangovers. While such subsistence fishing was a far cry from sportfishing as we know it today, these Friday morning treks had nonetheless made a strong impression on my father who was eager to accompany his mother. These enthusiastic impressions were further ingrained by Mr. Geresin, a teacher who was temporarily living with my father's family. He tempted my father with after-school fishing trips. For any typical boy, there would have been no conflict but my grandfather was a very religious man who believed that all spare time should be spent studying holy books and Jewish Law. Each time my dad went fishing, he got severely punished. As he says it, "I knew I would get the living daylights beat out of me, but I went anyway."

In the late 1920s, political rumblings were cause for great concern. Rona de Jos was in Transylvania, a region of Romania that was originally part of the Hungarian Empire. Romania had seized it and now Hungary wanted it back. This sent shock waves through Jewish shtetls (small Jewish communities) as Jews were often forced into front-line duty during wartime, then ruthlessly discarded when of no further use to the army. At the same time, an Austrian corporal, Adolph Hitler, laughed at only a few years earlier, was slow-

ly building his Nazi machine which among other things, promised to rid Germany and all of Europe of its Jews. After constant pleading, my grandmother finally convinced my grandfather to come to America. He came in 1931 and the rest of the family followed in 1934. A tradition of fishing would have to be practiced some place else.

After eight days of vomiting, the ordeal of Ellis Island, and a bumpy bus ride, the family ended up in Middletown, Ohio, a place where my grandfather, a rabbi, was able to find a pulpit. It was here that a very patient, dedicated, and giving teacher, Mrs. Wright, taught my father how to read, write, and speak English. There was really not much of an opportunity to fish in Middletown, but the seed had been planted. After only three years in Middletown, the family moved north to Cleveland where the benefits of a large city and a significantly larger Jewish community would benefit the entire family, especially my grandfather who longed to be in the company of other great scholars like himself. As for my father, a tradition of fishing would have to be practiced someplace else.

After art school, military service in World War II, and a variety of odd jobs, my father settled down with my mother in a suburb outside of Cleveland. With growing economic freedom, the lure of fishing became a ritual practiced "religiously" on weekends and once a year on a trip to Canada.

Somewhere along the way, I arrived on the scene, partaking in the weekly and yearly expeditions. The fishing left its mark but so did the ethics and values that went along with it.

When I was seven, we saw an advertisement in the *Cleveland Plain Dealer* about a new trout lake that was being opened to the public. Now one must understand that trout in Northeastern Ohio were precious, temporary, expensive, and not very accessible. If you wanted trout, you paid a lot of money for the right to fish them and even more money for the right to keep them. With great enthusiasm, we got up early one Sunday morning and drove to the lake which had been portrayed in the newspaper as a scenic natural body of water. As we drove by, we were greeted by nothing more than a large chocolate brown mudhole of no more than one acre. Quite obviously, it had been hastily dug out on the side of the road into which perhaps two hundred hatchery rainbows were dumped the previous day.

The "lake" was lined by anglers, each having paid $5.00 for the right to dip a bamboo pole with a piece of mono tied to the end. Being so young, I simply did not know what to think. I did want to fish. My father turned the car around and we drove home.

When fishing with my father, I was never really told to do this or that but several important fishing ethics and values were modelled. These form the foundation of my sportfishing philosophy. First and foremost, is that fishing in anything other than a natural setting is not sportfishing. Second, it is the pursuit of quarry, not the acquisition of dead fish that makes fishing so enjoyable. Third, fishing in unfair advantage is not sportfishing. Clearly, *challenge* is a necessary condition for sportfishing. Finally, fish should only be killed in numbers to the extent that eating one's catch remains something special. The sum of these ethics and values is what I call "the spirit of angling."

For every angler, there is perhaps a "moment of recognition," a point in time in which we realize that a technique of fishing or species of fish is special to us in a way that influences our life for a long time, if not forever. For me, that fateful time occurred on a bitterly cold December morning on a Lake Michigan pier. I was casting a shallow-diving bass plug into 33-degree water when a savage strike resulted in a battle I was totally not expecting nor prepared for. With the help of my close friend, a six-pound steelhead was landed. The fight was exciting, exhilarating but little did I realize the long-term effect that this experience would have on my life.

I had planned a career in academia: a professor at a major university, teaching psychology. But, as I got closer and closer to completing my Ph.D., I began to realize that fishing, especially fishing for steelhead and salmon, was the burning passion that I had to pursue. And while I may not be the world's best salmon or trout angler, it is the thing that I do best.

A lot of anglers and friends come into my office and see a B.A., M.Ed., and Ph.D. hanging on the wall. A few brave ones ask: "You spent ten years working for advanced degrees. Do you now feel that it was a waste?" I have two responses. First, maybe I needed to go through all that to reach the point I am at now. Being as happy as I am now, wouldn't that have been a tragedy not to have known, not to have found out? Second: what is education? Yes, it teaches you skills and practical things you need to know but much much more importantly, it teaches you how to live . . . how to be open-minded to new ideas, how to look at old ideas in new ways. It teaches you how to be a student of life. And if you ask me what my greatest asset as an angler is, I will tell you that it is my ability to ask the important questions, question the old beliefs, and believe that a higher level of understanding of fishing is always possible.

Read on. You will no doubt make a judgement as to how good of an angler I am. But if your judgement is favorable, please remember that from my point of view, it is *education* and my attitude towards it that made my techniques successful.

It is now late in the day. I look out of my window and see a setting Oregon sun paint large fir trees with a golden hue. My wife and I love it here in Oregon. The rivers, the high lakes, open country, uncrowded. It is all such a dream, a pot of gold at the end of the rainbow, and especially for someone who grew up in Northeast Ohio. And yet, I feel a certain restlessness . . . a restlessness to see and experience all I can in the world of steelhead, salmon and trout. I long to fish for salmon in Puget Sound, to explore a rejuvenated Lake Washington. Trolling for browns in early spring on Lake Ontario? That captures my imagination. And then there is my ultimate fantasy: to lead a team of American anglers to explore and document the rivers that hold Russian steelhead. Who knows where we will be ten years from now. However, one thing is clear: A tradition of fishing will have to be practiced someplace else.

Jed Davis
June 22, 1985

Battling a feisty chinook on Michigan's Pere Marquette. Sheldon Cohen photo

Contents

Dedication

This book is dedicated to all fishermen who understand and practice the "spirit of angling."

Chapter 1

Introduction and Overview

Methods and Myths

MANY DEVOTED STEELHEAD ANGLERS WOULD state, without hesitation, that drift fishing is the most productive technique for catching steelhead. Years ago, I would have nodded in agreement, not giving the subject a second thought. Over the last eight or ten years, I began to watch small but dedicated fraternities of nonconventional anglers perform their magic on steelhead, and with each new discovery, my views on "the most effective method" began to slowly fade. The final coup de grace occurred as I, too, began to achieve results with less conventional methods which for so many years I not only ignored but which I also regarded as marginal in terms of their relative effectiveness.

Consider, if you will, some nonconventional steelhead anglers, their techniques, and the results they have achieved. For instance, I cannot imagine a drift fisherman consistently outfishing fly angler Bill McMillan on Washington's Washougal. Emil Dean achieves excellent results with his "drop-back" method on Michigan's St. Joseph. To many streamside snickers and sneers, the late Al Knudson would throw his softball-sized Marabou streamers into the high, off-colored waters of the Stillaguamish and Skagit rivers only to make some magnificent catches over the many years he devoted to steelhead fly fishing. In each case, these anglers employ a method fished by relatively few steelheaders and yet, in terms of angling success, probably less than ten percent of all steelhead enthusiasts could match the outstanding results that these anglers achieved year after year.

The inevitable response to these anglers and their success is "Why?" The answer to this question is the very point of this section.

I am of the opinion that no one technique is the most effective for taking steelhead. In fact, success has little to do with what general class of terminal tackle is tied to the end of your line — be it a drift bobber, fly, lure, or eggs. What success is ultimately dependent upon is how much you commit yourself to and perfect any one method you choose to fish. This is the key! The classic historical example of this view is A. H. E. Wood and his development of the greased line fly technique for Scotland's Atlantic salmon. Here was a man whose love for fly fishing and dogged determination to solve various angling problems and salmon mysteries led to one of the greatest success stories in the history of angling. What's more, he would not be diverted or discouraged because of failure. Lack of success only served to increase his curiosity and determination.

At this point in the discussion, one may ask: "What does all this have to do with steelhead spinner fishing?" Simply, so many books and articles are written as if they are a cure-all for one's fishing ills. That is, fishing authors tend to speak in glowing terms, conveying a feeling that "if you read this book, you will catch more fish." Of course, suggestions of this sort are aided by the angler himself who very much *wants* to believe that he has found *the* answer. Over the years, I, like hundreds of other anglers, have been aided by countless books and articles on fishing but in each case, as I followed each and every direction, I soon realized that the knowledge carried to the stream was only a starting point; that what I had read was perhaps a means to an end but not an end in itself and that real expertise could only come from considerable experimentation accompanied by a fair share of frustration.

I love to catch steelhead, salmon and trout with spinners and, as you read through the chapters of this book, you will no doubt sense my enthusiasm. You may also think that I am making it all look so easy and, that in fact, spinner fishing for these species is an easy technique to learn. I must admit, that at this point in my career, I do not find it particularly difficult to catch a steelhead or salmon on a spinner. Whether fishing for winter or summer fish, in normal conditions and in fishable numbers, I expect to catch two or more fish on every trip out. But please remember it took a long time to get to this point. When I decided that I wanted to seriously give spinners a try, it took some twenty trips before I hooked my first fish. Then there was a time when I only got a fish on every fourth or fifth trip. But I stuck with it, determined to develop the technique to the point where I could consistently hook fish.

Although spinners were always a part of my repertoire of techniques, I had been primarily a drift fisherman for a number of years prior to using spinners exclusively and thus had to learn how to read water for spinners, not to mention develop different spinners for different water and prevailing light conditions. Needless to say, there were many obstacles along the way which included anglers themselves. For example, when I moved to Oregon, I had had no experience with summer steelhead as, at that time, Michigan had not yet started their summer-run program. I became fascinated with the fact that summer steelhead seemed to turn off as soon as the sun hit the water and I became obsessed with the prospect of catching summer-runs under cloudless skies. Among others, one local outdoor writer and "steelhead expert" told me not to waste my time trying to catch summer-runs in bright sunshine and suggested that if I was intent on catching big fish in direct sunlight, that I join him for carp fishing at some of the local man-made reservoirs. As it turned out, I now take more summer-runs in direct sunlight than I do in any other conditions.

The author with two early summer-runs taken in the lower McKenzie. David Davis photo

This leads to a very important point. This book is only a starting point for you, the angler. I have tried to discuss in as much detail as possible the elements that I think lead to successful spinner fishing for steelhead, salmon, and trout. But I also do it with the understanding that there is no substitute for actual stream experience. Like any other method, satisfying results can only be realized from being on the stream. Thus, unless you are an angler with lots of related experience — drift fishing and pulling plugs excluded — it would be unrealistic to assume that you can do well from the start. It's going to take lots of practice, a bit of patience, a strong commitment and, as with my own experience, it is likely to be accompanied by a fair degree of initial frustration. If you have made ten trips without a hit, I would understand if you sent threatening letters. But even so, you'll be better off than I was. I simply had no one to send letters to.

Overview of Book

This book is, first and foremost, a book on spinner fishing for steelhead. In fact, up until Chapter 12, I make very little reference to salmon and trout. In steelhead, we have a gamefish that is quickly becoming one of the most highly prized gamefishes in North America. While the primary and most diverse steelhead fishery exists in the Pacific Northwest, the Great Lakes area also has an excellent fishery. Wild and hatchery steelhead abound in all five of the Great Lakes. The increasing recognition by Great Lakes fish and game officials of the steelhead's popularity has directed significant amounts of funds toward not only the propagation of hatchery stocks, but also to the protection of wild steelhead stocks in this region.

Like many steelheaders, I prefer to fish for steelhead over any other available fish. I go after steelhead at least one hundred days per year. My own personal image clearly lies with steelhead, hence the focus. The chapters on trout and salmon deal more with the uniqueness of these species relative to steelhead. I saw no point in repeating many of the concepts elaborated upon in the steelhead chapters. In the end, however, there are more similarities than dissimilarities with regard to technique. In a few instances, I purposely reserved discussion of a particular aspect of technique for the salmon and trout chapters because I felt it played a more vital role in the pursuit of trout and salmon. Thus, should you be only interested in one of the species discussed, it might be helpful to at least take a glance at the other chapters.

This book is primarily a book on river fishing for steelhead, salmon and trout. In Chapter 12, lake strategy and surf techniques are discussed but, by and large, the major focus is toward river fishing. There are two reasons for this. First, a good portion of serious cold-water fishing takes place on rivers. This isn't to say that there are no well-developed techniques for lake or surf fishing. Quite to the contrary. In Michigan, we had a number of salmon and trout anglers who were devoted to the surf, their technique and precision being as complex and delicate as anyone would find with river fishing. However, relatively few anglers have gravitated to these techniques. Quite frankly, there is not the interest that one finds with river fishing. The second reason for dealing primarily with river fishing has to do with personal values. I simply have no interest in trolling for Spring Chinook at the mouth of Oregon's Clackamas or in trolling for Skamania-strain summer steelhead in southern Lake Michigan. What's more, if my heart isn't in it, I can't conscientiously write about it because, in the end, my writing would be based on someone else's experience and I have no way of verifying its accuracy.

In setting out to write this book, I had a number of goals. The first was to treat steelhead spinner fishing as a total method. What I mean by this is that the selection of spinners and development of casting skills cannot be separated from other aspects of technique such as reading water and knowing what steelhead will hit given a set of river and weather conditions. My criticism of most books on fishing technique is that far too much emphasis is placed on terminal tackle. I am all for the right lures, baits and flies but, as I have found out over the years, this is only half the story. Great spinners offer no advantage if you don't know when and where to fish them. In every chapter that addresses technique, you will take note of the fact that I go into great detail about environmental factors related to steelhead, salmon and trout before I even touch on spinner selection. From my point of view, you cannot become a true expert unless your decisions about where to fish, when, and how are based on a knowledge of things like water temperature, available lighting, water clarity, and water surface, as well as other factors. Looking into your tackle box and picking a lure based on a hunch can only lead to *random fishing* success because only by chance will lure be matched to conditions and corresponding fish behavior.

A second goal was related to the first goal; that is, I wanted to present a somewhat scientific or systematic strategy for pursuing steelhead, salmon and trout with spinners. This strategy, or as I like to call it, "fishing within a framework," is not something I concocted on paper from behind my desk. This is how I found I could become the most successful. This is how I approach my cold-water fishing on a day-to-day basis. A lot of anglers see the steelhead as somewhat of a mystery and they delegate their success or lack of it to fate or the nature of steelheading. I used to believe this myself but when I began to discipline myself toward fishing with a strategy, I discovered steelhead to be quite predictable. As I understood this predictability more and more, the fish became progressively easier to catch. I now catch more steelhead than I ever dreamed was possible.

The third goal was to explain, in detail, technical information about how to make spinners and where to buy parts. From the letters and phone calls received via my magazine articles, I realized that there was a real thirst for knowledge. The spinner is the world's most popular lure and, yet, so little has been written on the subject. Unfortunately, many of the most desirable spinner parts can only be found via mail-order. What's more, some of my most important materials come from firms that have nothing to do with the fishing industry per se. One could quite literally go crazy trying to find certain parts that they saw some tight-lipped angler successfully use. I guess that my first inclination was to keep all of my sources a secret but then what good would

A feisty steelie sends a spray of water into the sunlight. Asa Pearl photo

writing a book be? People become upset, discouraged and ultimately lose interest when they can't find something they need.

And, maybe this latter point hints of my most important goal. I truly enjoy taking steelhead, salmon and trout on spinners. I have fished all methods and none offers as much personal satisfaction as spinner fishing. I want others to discover just how much fun it is, how exciting it is and how much there is to it. For this reason, *I have held nothing back.* Everything I know about spinner fishing is discussed in this book. Stick with it for awhile, friends. The more you fish this method, the more you'll like it — and you just might discover, as I have, that spinner fishing can be a very effective technique for taking steelhead, salmon and trout.

Chapter 2

Fishing Spinners Within a Framework

Setting a Framework

EVERY FISHERMAN HAS HAD THE EXPERIENCE of seeing many different sizes and colors of lures displayed on the shelf of a sporting goods store. While the selection is usually impressive, how do you, the angler, decide which lure will best suit the lake or stream conditions you intend to fish? It is my opinion that lure selection, for most anglers, has always been a haphazard or random affair based on hearsay, conditioning, superstition, or even eye-appeal. What I think happens to most anglers is the following: The fisherman selects lures "X," "Y," and "Z." Through rotation, he eventually makes a satisfying catch and concludes that he has found the "right one." He now confidently fishes the *chosen lure*, taking a fish here and there and, once or twice a season, an outstanding catch is made. He then concludes that when the fish are "biting," he has got the secret weapon.

My understanding of these classic situations is a bit different. In reality the angler only makes good catches when his favored lure coincides with conditions that are best suited to his particular lure and style of fishing. The result is then a predictable one. Sometimes he gets skunked, sometimes he catches a fish, and once in a great while, he makes a really fine catch — the saga of the American Fisherman.

The above description is typical of anglers who fish lures for steelhead. But, this need not be the case. I believe that one of the reasons spinner fishing for steelhead has never been taken that seriously is because few anglers have ever taken the scientific approach to fishing them; that is, the matching of lure to prevailing conditions as does the fly fisherman who typically carries one or two dozen different fly patterns to the stream.

Furthermore, I also believe that somehow, anglers have always believed that if a fish is going to take hardware (spinner or spoon), size, color, degree of flash, in relation to light conditions, water color, and water temperature was not that important of a consideration. Thus, it comes as no surprise when I see two fellows going after summer steelhead with 1/4- and 1/2-ounce silver Stee-lees in bright sunshine and gin clear water, with a temperature of 56°. Such an endeavor may provide relaxation but, rarely, will this combination produce good fishing!

The purpose here is to put spinner fishing for steelhead within a scientific framework, one in which choice of a particular spinner is based on tangible environmental factors. This will dictate what size, color, and weight spinner should be used. Outside of certain environmental extremes, i. e., very warm water, extremely low water, etc., there is absolutely no reason why steelhead cannot be negotiated with spinners on a consistent basis in all conditions. All one needs is a bit of patience, a considerable amount of practice, and a simple but accurate thermometer with which to measure water temperature.

The framework I intend to discuss throughout this book is one I began to develop during my last years in Michigan. However, the major consolidation of my method took place while living in Eugene, Oregon. I was fortunate to have lived only 25 minutes from my favorite McKenzie River drifts which during weekdays (the only time I fish) were deserted. During the course of the season, I would bear witness to dramatic changes in water temperature and water levels. It became a challenge to take steelhead in all conditions. I also found various flats, pools, and tailouts which held good numbers of steelhead. In fact, in one spot I called the "Booby Flats," it was not uncommon to hook three steelhead in three casts. The importance of the solitude and exclusivity I enjoyed on "my" particular drifts cannot be underestimated. On each day I drifted from mid-summer on, while experimenting with different spinners, I knew that failure to get a strike was *not* a result of extra-angler interference or competition but, rather, the result of my failure to discover the right combination to match the prevailing conditions. It was a unique opportunity! Thus, it wasn't long before I started solving some of the challenges posed by seemingly unfavorable conditions. On some days I would start out using a large No. 4 silver spinner adorned with chartreuse tape and tail, only to switch to a No. 2 spinner with a solid black blade and purposely-tarnished brass body.

From our home in Eugene, I was also fortunate enough to be within reasonable driving distance of the South Umpqua, South and North Santiam, Siuslaw and its North Fork, Alsea, and Lake Creek. While some of these rivers are better spinner rivers than others, they all provide at least some opportunity for the spinner fisherman. And, while I spent far more time on the McKenzie due to the length of the season and its proximity, I found that the framework developed worked with the same predictability on all rivers I fished.

I also think it important to mention that, while the framework to be discussed is original in terms of its application to spinners, similar frameworks have been applied to fly fishing for steelhead and Atlantic salmon. In that regard, much of my initial experimentation was inspired by Jock Scott's classic *Greased Line Fishing for Salmon* in which Arthur Wood's technique for taking salmon in low water and bright sunshine is discussed. Also influential was a 1974 four-part series of articles appearing in *Salmon Trout Steelheader* magazine. Author Bill McMillan, fly fisherman extraordinaire, and undisputed "Wizard of the Washougal," most eloquently described his approach for taking steelhead in each of the four seasons. Perhaps the greatest influence of all were answers to questions I posed to Bill via the mail. His well-thought-out and brilliantly-stated responses, not to mention his beautiful handwriting, were a delight and an inspiration to continue my search and conceptualization.

In some ways, I see my experimentation only as an application of principles discovered years before I was born. Thus, I don't want to leave an impression that what I have written is revolutionary. However, the application to spinners and spin fishing is something that has not yet been explored in great depth in either magazines or a book.

Why Spinners Over Other Lures?

There are a number of classes of weighted artificial lures that can be used by the spin fisherman — spoons, wobblers, jigs, soft plastics, spinner baits, and, of course, spinners. Why, then, do I choose to fish spinners over other lure types? There are three reasons: **effectiveness, versatility, unlimited design possibilities**. Let's take a look at each.

When a well-designed spinner, matched to prevailing conditions, is being fished properly, I feel that, in general, no other lure can beat its fish-catching qualities. There is something about a blade spinning around a shaft that induces fish to strike. Anyone who has given the spinner a good chance knows this but who can explain why? After all, what is a spinner? It doesn't imitate a fish; it doesn't look like an aquatic animal; and yet, it continues to be a wonder lure. No one will argue this point. Of all artificial

baits that I ever fished, none do I fish with as much confidence as a spinner. I believe in spinners and the more I fish them, the more my confidence in them grows.

The spinner is **the** most versatile lure known to the spin fisherman. It can be fished fast, slow, shallow, or deep. Too much current does not ruin its effectiveness and, when properly designed, it can be fished very slowly without any loss in its fish-catching ability. Too fast of a current renders spoons and wobblers ineffective. Furthermore, a fair amount of tension or current is necessary to get them to work properly. This does not mean that spinners are necessarily easier to fish . . . they aren't! Bouncing a Stee-lee off the bottom of a prime steelhead lie is much easier than doing the same thing with a spinner. The important point is that, with practice, there is a potential for effectively fishing spinners in all types of water.

I practice the sport of steelhead fishing in a very scientific and systematic way. I simply don't look in my tackle box and select spinners on a hunch. Every single aspect of spinner design — be it size, color, degree of flash, or adornments — has a specific purpose. Because a spinner is made of so many parts and because these many parts are so readily available, there exists an almost limitless array of design possibilities. This is not the case with the spinner's biggest competitors — spoons and wobblers. A spoon is stamped on a metal stamping machine. Thus, the angler is forced to go with a limited number of available designs. Now it is true that you can make your own wood dies and pound out spoon shapes, but this involves considerable work and can never achieve the same precision that can be attained via metal stamping.

A Summer Green took this North Santiam steelhead. The hooked nose hints of the Washougal strain, of which the Skamania is part. Jed Davis photo

Wobblers are injection-molded by machines that cost hundreds of thousands of dollars. Thus, once again, the angler must work with a limited number of body styles and sizes. If an angler has confidence in lures other than spinners, I will be the last one to tell him he should fish spinners. But, just the same, I would probably be one of the last fishermen to give up spinners. Experience has told me that they are an incredibly effective and reliable bait. No wonder they are the world's most popular artificial lure!

Spinner as Attractor

In order to systematically determine how and why a particular spinner is chosen to fish with on a given day, I feel that it is paramount to understand, at least from my point of view, what a spinner is . . . and what it is *not*. Being the single-most popular fishing lure in the world, thousands of theories have been concocted by as many anglers, and as long as someone is catching fish, it's hard to dismiss even the most zany point of view. The point is this: No one can ever really know for sure what the spinner portrays. I'll make my own case with the understanding that by some anglers' estimations, I could be totally off-track.

The spinner is most commonly thought of by most *other* anglers as a forage fish. With the majority of commercially-made spinners exhibiting a bright silver, nickel or brass blade, the bright flashing movement is thought to be related to the streaking of a minnow through the water — hence, the obvious link. *From my point of view, the spinner has got nothing at all to do with fish.* Different techniques give credence to this belief.

First, let's look at hotshotting for steelhead. This is a common technique employed in the Northwest and, as of late, is really starting to take off in the Great Lakes. Briefly, the method employs a deep-diving minnow-like wobbler that is back-trolled very slowly through steelhead-holding water. By holding the boat against the current with either oars or motor, the current takes the plug down to the bottom-hugging steelhead. The key to plug selection is matching the plug color to prevailing light conditions. The general rule most seasoned anglers fish by is this: dark colors in dark light; bright colors in sunny conditions; medium-toned plug colors in medium light. (The exception is high, dark, dirty water in which fluorescent colors are used for visibility.) Thus, when I hotshot the very popular Wee-Wart, I use a silver plug in bright sunshine, gold in high clouds, green in low dark clouds, and blue and purple in dense fog, at dawn, or at dusk. Interestingly, this same formula is generally used to troll the big waters of the Great Lakes for salmon and trout.

Why does this general pattern prevail? Very simply because a forage fish, or any fish for that matter, can only reflect as much light as there is available. None of the fish that enter our Northwest or Midwest streams have night-time fluorescent elements in their pigments. As a plug works down into the territory of a resting steelhead, artificially-induced high visibility lures have an unnatural appearance when fished in low light and are thus less effective strike provokers.

This phenomenon holds true for surface largemouth bass fishing. Two of the most popular surface lures ever invented are the Jitterbug and Hula Popper, both by Fred Arbogast Co. Both of these lures are available in nighttime fluorescent, frog, and black finishes. Interestingly, black is most effective in the dark, frog in the daytime. My Dad and I always joked that the fluorescent colors were excellent "fishermen catchers," but were otherwise rather worthless. Now, it is true, that while the surface movement and sonic attraction of these lures is more suggestive of a frog than a minnow, it nonetheless shows that freshwater creatures are more attractive to predators when presented such that their pigment makes a natural presentation of light reflection.

An obvious contradiction to these situations would be the success of the Dandy-Glo lure developed for salmon trolling in low light and dark conditions. The Dandy-Glo looks and behaves like some of the more popular forage-fish imitation trollers, such as the J-Plug, the main difference being that it has a bright fluorescent element placed in the transparent body which causes the lure to glow like a light bulb. If a Dandy-Glo catches fish, doesn't this fact defeat the belief that when fishing forage-fish imitations, dark colors should be used in dark lighting situations, etc.? No! In my opinion, a Dandy-Glo is not posing as a highly-visible forage fish but rather as an *attractor*. It is much the same difference when comparing a Glo-Go to eggs. Both are of similar size and both are fished in the same way. However, a Glo-Go is an attractor. Why? Have you ever seen red and white or pearl-pink fish eggs that spin madly as they float downstream?

Thus, we see that in many instances, the forage-fish imitations are most effective when they reflect light in a way not unlike that of the real thing. Why, then, do I not think the spinner to be a suggestion of a forage fish? Because, if, in fact, the spinner was a forage fish, it would follow the same general rules of matching lure color to prevailing light conditions as is the case with minnow imitations. The fact is that in fishing spinners for steelhead, I use a strategy which is the *exact opposite* of the one used for wobblers, diving plugs, and minnow imitations. That is, in general, the darker the light conditions, the brighter I go. For example, I might use a brass No. 3 for summer-runs if there is total cloud cover. As soon as the sun hits the water, I usually will go with a plain, smaller-sized brass that has been purposely tarnished. If the sun stays out, I almost always go with a black blade and body. Now, of course, there are other factors to consider, most notably water temperature, river stage height, and underwater visibility which may alter spinner selection. But, in most normal summer conditions, I am continually rewarded with this strategy. And yet, if I were to pull plugs for summer-runs, I would use the color strategy elaborated upon for forage-fish imitations.

The second point against thinking of a spinner as a forage fish is the action of the spinner itself. Simply, a wobbler has a side-to-side movement as does a fish. The spinner stays on a straight trajectory with the blade rapidly rotating. However, the point could be made that streamer flies, which are meant to imitate minnows, also move on a straight trajectory, as does the spinner, darting on a straight trajectory with a pull of the rod tip. I would respond by saying: First, a fly has no rotating blade; the key to any spinner is its blade. Second, many streamers, especially the very popular Muddler Minnow, are designed to pulsate in the water — not nearly to the degree of a wobbler, but nonetheless, to a degree.

The question then becomes this: What is the spinner portraying? There is no sure way of knowing but I will offer my opinion.

I view the spinner as an *attractor*. This has got nothing to do with what fish are in the river. It has to do with the fact that a spinner blade rotating about a shaft *excites* steelhead. The word "excite" can mean many different things such as provoke, anger, arouse curiosity, trigger playfulness, threaten, hypnotize, create a suggestion of life which is too good of a thing not to pass up, or invade territory. It will probably never be quite clear what this word means because steelhead do not talk. However, we can be sure that, for whatever reasons, steelhead are drawn to spinners.

When I build a spinner from the many parts available, I generally do not have any specific creature in mind that I am trying to imitate. I could not care less about trying to imitate anything in the aquatic environment of the steelhead. And even if I were trying to imitate something, it would be difficult because in or out of the water, the spinner does not closely resemble anything living under water. I am simply striving to develop an attractor that, for whatever reason, is attractive enough so that the steelhead will chase it and then strike. Mind you, I did not say "attack" or "eat" because I am not sure of the fish's motives. This is a key point because to develop spinners for steelhead, one has to free himself from the thought of "food." This is because you are not necessarily offering food. Thus, trying to imitate a squawfish, sea-run cutthroat, resident rainbow, or crawfish may prove to be a worthless venture. An attractor is simply an attractor — it does not necessarily have anything to do with food.

To further drive home this point, let's discuss relevant human analogies. One is advertising. Take a look at any supermarket shelf. There you see dozens of items packaged in attractive wrappings. Many of the packages are brightly or unusually shaped. Lettering varies. In short, various schemes are utilized to draw your attention to the available items. Every last line and color was purposely designed to attract your attention in the hope that you will pick up the item. If the packaging, as an attractor, appeals to you, there is an excellent chance that you will select it over other products. Ah! You have been hooked. Fish-on!

Likewise, steelhead are attracted to spinners because they are attractive. This may very well be exclusive of food, territorial threats, etc., and in the development and design of various patterns, it is wise to use "attraction" as the primary basis for construction.

I think that a good comparison may be drawn between steelhead flies and steelhead spinners in that both are built with attraction as the goal. An all-time favorite such as the "Skunk" vaguely resembles an aquatic invertebrate but nonetheless has qualities about it that would insult any respectable river-going nymph. And yet, thousands of steelhead are caught on this fly every year. Thor, Silver Hilton, Skykomish — all of these patterns are attractors — nothing else.

Threshold of Attraction

The answer to the question of "what makes a spinner optimally attractive" is the very core that determines what particular spinner is fished under a set of given conditions.

For steelhead spinner fishermen, attraction means exciting a fish to strike to the point of almost spooking it. The goal is this: How much glitter and flash, etc. can the fish stand before it is turned off. There is a threshold and, given the prevailing light conditions, water color, water depth, and boat traffic, I always strive to reach that threshold. Why? Because by providing an offering that flashes, shines, and glitters as much as the fish will tolerate, we stand the

greatest chance of *exciting* those fish present as well as attracting the attention of fish that are not in the direct path of the spinner but which nonetheless are in the general vicinity of the lure. It is these "peripheral" fish, those not in the direct path of the spinner, that we are most concerned about. If our spinner has enough flash to attract their attention and also excite them, then even if our lure does not come within two feet of their mouth, they will still be induced to move for the spinner and strike. Thus, spinner selection strives to

Negotiating white water is part of the fun of steelheading from a drift boat. Asa Pearl photo

provide as much flash as those fish present will stand which has the benefit of attracting steelhead from considerable distances outside the lure's path. Thus, reaching the *threshold of attraction* is the very thing that so often spells the difference between success and failure. Practically speaking, steelhead are not in great abundance in most streams. In a one-mile stretch of a typical stream, we may pass over only four or five fish. By having a lure that can effectively attract from a large radius, the chances are greatly improved for attracting and negotiating those fish available.

A practical example demonstrates just how important the threshold of attraction is. The lowest drift on Oregon's Siuslaw is referred to as the "Willows." It is a very popular drift, easily negotiated with a boat, and, at times, loaded with steelhead. The drift gets its name from a section of water midway through the drift that is shallow, full of protruding willows, and marked by dozens of miniature tailouts, pools, pockets, and terraces. On approaching this section, a break extends the full length of the river. On the right side, a fairly deep slot and pool can be identified with a pair of polarized sunglasses. While most boats pass it up, a few anglers throw their assorted hardware into the slot in the hope of hooking a fish. During a March 1982 drift, I observed two anglers anchored adjacent to the slot for one-half hour while eating their lunch in between casts. I was working some water a quarter mile upstream hoping they would move on, when I finally approached. They finally did move over the break and began fishing the Willows. I anchored in their spot and much to their amazement, I hooked and landed a steelhead on the first cast.

Why did this happen? This particular holding water is a very narrow and deep V-shaped slot and, for protection, the fish lie in the lowest spot. It is virtually impossible to run your lure directly in their path. Any offering must be passed one or two feet above the fish. Obviously, a fish will have to be induced to move for the bait. The Stee-lees these anglers were using were nickel-plated on one side and red and white painted on the other side. This is a very popular lure which, no doubt, has taken thousands of fish every year; but, next to the No. 4 silver-plated spinner I was using with its fluorescent tubing and tape, the Stee-lee does not look like much of an attention-getter. Let's compare. Nickel gives off a much darker flash in the water than does genuine silver. The red and white paints used on Stee-lees do not have daylight fluorescent elements in their pigments as does the tubing I use on the hook shank or the tape I use on the spinner blade, not to mention the sonic attraction of the spinner itself. The net result is that the Stee-less cannot attract and excite from as great a distance as does the spinner. This is why I got the fish with one cast whereas the lunching anglers missed with fifty casts. Had the steelhead I caught been resting in more easily negotiable water, it is likely that these anglers would have gotten the strike. In many cases, those in which the lure drifts directly in the path of the fish, it probably does not matter whether your offering is brass, nickel, silver, raw steel, or fluorescent painted. But there are also many cases where steelhead must be teased or excited from their lair. It is these cases where attaining the threshold of attraction can make a very significant difference.

But just as there are cases where it takes a great deal of flash and glitter to induce the fish into striking, there are also cases where it takes very little. I fish stretches of water where I use a No. 1 black blade with a black body to hook steelhead. Anything larger or brighter spooks the fish.

Remember that in a steelhead's upstream journey, he has two major concerns: rest and safety. In the ocean, the steelhead enjoyed a seemingly limitless area to roam in, enjoying comfortable depths of 20 to 100 feet of water. Upon entering a stream above tidewater, he must now expose himself to depths of 18 inches to six feet. No wonder these fish are so wary! Therefore, in presenting an offering, one must be careful not to violate the fish's sense of security.

The threshold of attraction is then that point where the largest and gaudiest offering can be successfully presented to the fish at short distances but which will also attract fish from the greatest radius possible. Finding this threshold is a key to good steelhead spinner fishing. Is it necessary to reach this threshold of attraction in order to be successful? Absolutely not — but it helps. Let me explain via example. Under conditions "X," I may know that a No. 3 brass spinner is the "limit" and that use of anything larger or gaudier will spook fish. Now let's say I lose my last No. 3 brass and only have No. 2 brass spinners left. Can I still catch fish? Yes, but because the No. 2 is smaller, it will not excite the fish from as great a distance, as would a No. 3. As a result, I may fail to induce certain fish to chase the No. 2 which probably would have chased the No. 3. Thus, my chances for success could be reduced.

The threshold of attraction can only be determined through streamside experience and experimentation. Just as steelheaders read water to locate good holding water, the spinner fisherman must learn to read water for spinner selection. While I discuss this in later chapters from a practical point of view as well as explain which spinner combinations have worked well for me for winter and summer steelhead, it is important to note that there is no substitute for streamside experience. This will involve paying close attention to water height, temperature, clarity and available lighting. At first, you may feel lost; but, with a season or two of concentration and dedication, you may just start approaching streams with a high degree of confidence . . . and leaving the stream with some rewarding experiences.

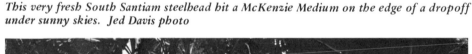

This very fresh South Santiam steelhead bit a McKenzie Medium on the edge of a dropoff under sunny skies. Jed Davis photo

Chapter 3

Building and Buying Spinners

A S MENTIONED EARLIER, A LOT OF ANGLERS feel that if a steelhead is going to take a lure, color, size, and degree of flash are not very important considerations. I wish this were true. Then I could fish one spinner all year and never have to second-guess my choice. Unfortunately, the experience of other steelhead spinner fishermen and myself shows this not to be the case. Spinner selection is extremely critical to consistent success. The person who wants to seriously fish spinners for steelhead, and especially for summer steelhead, is going to have to keep an assortment of different spinners handy for varying conditions. Knowing how to properly build spinners or knowing what to look for when buying commercially-produced spinners is an important primary consideration.

Building Versus Buying

It would be nice if we could drop into a nearby tackle shop and buy ready-made steelhead spinners for the price of a drift bobber — but it just isn't possible. The heavy premium metals needed for weighting plus the labor involved in having someone assemble the spinner drives the price right through the ceiling. Actually, the price laid out for one spinner is not prohibitive. Any angler who spends $10.00 in gas to get to his favorite stream can certainly afford a $3.00 lure. On a typical day, a good spinner fisherman will lose two to four spinners and sometimes six to eight. This is where the price becomes prohibitive and this is why most dedicated spinner fishermen make their own spinners. Buying components in quantities of a hundred or a thousand, I can make large winter steelhead spinners for under $1.00 and smaller ones for under thirty-five cents. At this price, I can well afford to lose four to six spinners a day. And if you compare homemade spinner loss with terminal tackle that drift fishermen lose, the cost is about the same.

There is also an additional consideration related to the above issue that nearly every angler has encountered. That is, when an angler buys an expensive piece of terminal tackle, he becomes afraid of losing it and, thus, begins to fish it protectively. As a result, effective presentation is sacrificed for protection against loss. *When you start fishing spinners to save the spinner, as opposed to fishing spinners to reach the fish, your chances for success are greatly reduced.* This is especially true for steelhead spinner fishing. As explained in later chapters, a spinner must be fished deep, close to structures, and cast into spots where no bottom bouncer or tackle-saving-minded angler would dare go. In fact, there are many times when I know my spinner has less than a fifty-fifty chance of surviving. But, if the holding water looks good, I would never pass it up. By making my own spinners, thereby cutting the cost dramatically, I am then psychologically freed from the "save-the-spinner syndrome" and can therefore fish each part of the river as I think it should be fished. The result is an obvious one: I catch more fish than the person "hung up with getting hung up."

Related to the above is yet another consideration. Rarely do I ever go after a spinner that I cannot pull loose. I generally spend no more than 20 seconds trying to free the spinner. If it won't release, I break the line and immediately tie on another spinner. Much to my partner's amazement, I have been doing this for years, but it is for a good reason. First, I like to be fishing, not chasing lures for ten minutes with a drift boat. My fishing time is too valuable to be concerned about a 75 cent investment. Besides, once a lure is snagged, there is no guarantee that, if I take the time to free it, I will actually get it. Second, retrieving a snagged lure often means drifting downstream. This may mean that I cannot row back to my original spot. And, even if I could row back, chances are I spooked the fish in the hole in trying to maneuver a boat and retrieve my spinner. Anyone who is frugal with their money is almost compelled to retrieve a $3.00 Mepps but if you can make the same type of lure considerably better for forty cents, your time and concentration can be directed to your primary purpose: to fish for steelhead.

Interestingly, there are times when I am afflicted by the save-the-spinner syndrome due to my own absent-mindedness. When I fish on two successive days, I sometimes forget to replenish my supply of spinners for the next day. Excited about the day ahead, I open my tackle box on the second day and am greeted by the sight of three spinners instead of eight. I am then forced to fish carefully or risk having nothing to fish with. Rarely, if ever, do I have really good days when this happens.

Are there any circumstances under which buying a ready-made spinner is preferable to making your own? Yes, I think so. If 30 percent or less of your fishing time is spent casting spinners, you are probably better off buying them. Aside from the fact that it is more convenient, you probably will not lose that many if you spend so little time fishing them. I know many anglers who are predominantly drift fishermen but who carry a few lures with them. Generally, they like to throw lures as a change of pace, or because there are a few good spots in their drifts which cannot be effectively fished with drift gear.

Finally, I think that in many cases, Northwest bank anglers are better off buying spinners. These anglers generally have limited river access and are confined to fishing a few spots along the river. They get to know these spots so well that they can pinpoint exactly where to fish their spinner and they know exactly where potential snags are.

Is there any compromise between buying and building? There are a number of mail-order houses that offer all the necessary components in quantities of ten. For under ten dollars, you can build ten premium steelhead spinners. Such a modest investment should provide enough spinner fishing to tell you whether you want to pursue the technique any further.

The Importance of Proper Design

Over the years, I have developed preferences for the color and finish I use on my various spinners. For example, I depend heavily upon silver-plated spinners for winter steelhead but other anglers like brass or are perfectly happy with nickel. In regard to the aesthetic and cosmetic, this is totally a matter of what works for you. In fact, I would estimate that in some situations, ten different color and finish spinner combinations would do equally well. However, I do believe there to be certain basic guidelines that should be closely followed in regard to spinner construction. The reason for specific guidelines relates to the blade. A blade will not revolve around the spinner shaft if spacing, proportions, and weighting are not within certain limits and, unless that blade spins, the lure is almost totally ineffective. On a truly good spinner, getting the blade to spin is never a concern. It starts immediately upon retrieval, and yanks on the rod tip to start the blade are totally unnecessary. A good spinner doesn't need a fast retrieve or a fast-moving river current to get the blade to work. A good spinner blade spins dependably and at a snail's pace. The point is this: If you are now fishing a homemade or ready-made spinner which does not have the capabilities I just mentioned, it is time to redesign your own or look for another brand in your sports shop. Let me point out an example.

I feel that the Rooster-Tail line of spinners offered by Yakima Bait Co. offers a fantastic choice of color combinations to choose from. They offer just about every color imaginable. However, the clevis, which holds the blade to the shaft, is often too closely sandwiched between the eye and body. This prevents the blade from turning freely on the shaft. Add a folded clevis (which produces more friction than the preferred stirrup clevis) and a swing blade (which needs a lot of resistance to get it started relative to a "French"-type blade) and you have got one temperamental lure. Now it is true that Rooster Tails are very popular but you also hear scores of complaints about the blade from just about anyone who ever used one.

On occasion, I will start fishing a new spinner and quickly discover that I am having difficulty in getting the blade to consistently spin. Sometimes upon examination I can discover what the problem is. At other times I cannot, so I put it aside and rebuilt it at a later time. I simply cannot be bothered by a blade that spins erratically because there are too many other factors I need to pay attention to while fishing steelhead. If my concentration is diverted or if I have to alter my presentation because the blade will not work where and how I want it to work, then I am not fishing effectively.

An example illustrates the point. Several seasons back, I was testing a homemade spinner that had been sent to me by a person in Ohio. Early in my McKenzie River drift, I approached two protruding boulders which provided sanctuary to resting summer-runs. I had consistently hooked fish from this spot. I quartered the new spinner down to the hot spot but saw that the blade was not turning properly. I yanked on the rod tip to start the blade which in turn spooked a steelhead from its holding water. I could never be sure if the fish would have hit. I do know that a poorly designed spinner insured that I would never find out!

Basic Spinner Design Strategy

There are some suggested guidelines that should be followed when constructing a steelhead spinner. Slight variations from these guidelines do not dramatically change the

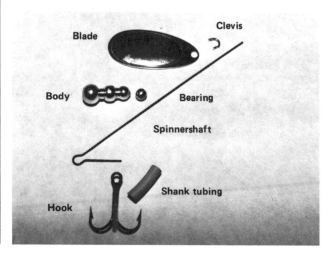

responsiveness of your spinner. Experience has shown that if you do pay attention to the various details outlined below, you probably will never have to worry about how a particular retrieve might affect your blade. Thus, you will be able to fish your spinner with confidence, knowing that it is fishing effectively 100 percent of the time. This, in turn, will allow you to focus your attention on getting the spinner to where the fish are.

Blade

In fishing spinners for steelhead, the angler is going to fish many different types of water in which speed and depth vary greatly. Many hard-to-get holding areas will be less than the size of a kitchen table. This means that the instant your spinner hits the water, it is going to have to start working. In short, the blade has to be responsive under a wide variety of conditions. Spinner blade designs are like bush pilots in Alaska and psychiatrists in Southern California — a dime a dozen.

There are so many blade designs available that I have lost track. However, one stands out as the most dependable and ideally suited for steelhead spinner fishing — the French-type blade. This famous domed blade is found on nearly all Mepps spinners. The patents on this wonder blade have long run out and a good percentage of spinners feature this same type of blade. While you may observe slight variations in design from one blade to the next, there is no need to be concerned. All French-type blades that have a .0247-in. or .032-in. gauge blade (see paragraph below) function quite satisfactorily. Mail-order houses listed at the end of this chapter offer these blades on a retail basis. There simply is no problem obtaining them. However, because of trademarks and copyrights, you will often see these blades called something other than "French-type" and "Mepps" blades. Names like "Spem," "Radar," and "American" are used in place of the famous names. The important thing to look for when ordering is the photo or drawing. These blades are easily identified.

In general, these blades are usually stamped in brass and offered in two different finishes — polished brass or nickel plate. As mentioned above, you might find that the shape or design differs slightly from one manufacturer to the next. This is not critical. What is critical is the gauge of the brass used to stamp the blade. Generally, three different gauges are used: .022-in., .0247-in., and .032-in. I highly recommend buying from a manufacturer who stamps on .032-in. gauge for three important reasons. First, a heavier blade adds weight to the lure. Most importantly though is that, as your spinner is working through water, its heavier gauge allows you to feel the blade spinning through pulsations on the tip of your rod. This is extremely valuable for the following reason. A spinner is most effective when the blade is rotating at a slow speed. If you can control for a slow blade speed, the spinner will provide the most flash and draw the most strikes. A slow blade spin will also create less resistance and allow the blade to work deeper. The .032-in. gauge blade is superior for this purpose. While the .022-in. and .0247-in. blades spin with the same ease, you will not feel the tap-tap-tap-tap on your rod tip. There is a third reason why I prefer the heavier gauge blade. Although the edge of the blade constitutes a tiny fraction of the total surface area, I find that the thicker .032-in. edge adds an extra amount of flash to the whole spinner.

Mail-order houses do not list the gauge of the brass used on their blades. You can write or call to find out or buy a sample and measure with a caliper.

Blade Length

Regardless of the blade you use, there is a simple rule that should be followed when constructing spinners. That is, the blade, when hanging on a spinner that is held upright, should extend at least the entire length of the body. Observation of this rule goes a long way in achieving the proper ratio of body weight to blade size. This, in turn, results in a spinner that will spin on command. On my spinners, I like the blade to extend slightly beyond the body, perhaps to the eye of the hook. I prefer this arrangement because of the feel it produces. However, I offer a bit of caution: Extension of the blade as described above does not

Blade should extend beyond body on a well-built spinner.

mean that you can then use an unlimited amount of weight in the body. Beyond a certain point, spinner responsiveness will decrease.

Clevis

The clevis holds the blade to the spinner shaft. Stirrup clevises are better than folded clevises because they produce less friction, thus letting the blade spin more freely on the shaft. Stirrup clevises are also sturdier and will not bend as easily. Stirrup clevises are more expensive but the difference between one style and the other is a small fraction of a penny.

Bearing

When using a solid brass body on the larger spinners, the clevis should rest on a tiny metal or plastic bearing that is positioned between body and clevis. The purpose here is to reduce friction on the clevis as much as possible. By providing a surface on which the clevis rests that has a minimum of surface area, the blade will spin more freely. On some smaller No. 1 and 2 spinners, the brass beads positioned next to the clevis are so small that no additional bearing is necessary.

Body

Because the French-type blade causes considerable resistance when spinning in the water, a fast-spinning blade which is often unavoidable in fast current causes the spinner to rise to the surface. Unless the water being worked is very shallow, this resistance will put it out of the steelhead's range. In order to compensate for this problem, it is desirable to weight spinners so they sink quickly and stay down. Solid brass beads and bodies are excellent for this purpose. The many available sizes and shapes are available in polished brass and nickel plate.

For winter steelhead, I silver plate brass bodies. When used in combination with a silver-plated blade, the spinner gives off the brightest possible flash. No spinner that I have ever seen, commercial or homemade, can come close to matching this spinner's flash.

A number of anglers like to use various-sized worm weights as bodies. They are ideal for this purpose but beyond a certain relative weight, they prevent the blade from rotating. Thus, if you desire maximum weighting, you will need to experiment with the different sizes available. It also must be noted that a lead worm weight has a very dull finish relative to brass, nickel, or genuine silver. They do not silver-plate very well in home plating operations so you might want to paint them. Spray-paint them in fluorescent colors, then coat with a clear, thin, two-part polymer used by rod builders for finishing rods. The polymer coat adds a nice gloss and virtually eliminates paint chip.

When constructing the larger spinners in sizes 3, 4, and 5, it is wise to stick with the heavier solid brass beads and bodies. Cut glass, hollow brass, and plastic beads look nice but they will not help you get down to the bottom-hugging steelhead. When fishing No. 1 and 2 spinners, which are usually used for summer steelhead in shallow riffles, weighting is not as critical, although use of appropriate solid brass beads will help you cast farther with less effort and with much greater accuracy. Because of their relative size, you will not have to worry about snagging bottom. In fact, I lose far fewer No. 1s and 2s than I do the larger-sized spinners.

The Perfect Balance

As we shall see in the following chapters, one of the real keys to a good spinner is 1) a body that allows the spinner to be well-weighted and 2) a blade that can be controlled for *slow-blade spin.* The sum of these qualities can be defined as "the perfect balance." If the spinner you are fishing lacks one or both of these qualities, your ability to fish with 100% effectiveness, which is our goal, will be almost impossible to achieve. Let's look at each point.

One of the problems of spinners in general is that by their basic design, they have weight restrictions. Beyond a certain body weight, spinners will not spin. Remember! Our primary goal is to have that spinner spin on command to the point where we don't even think about it. We can only use as much weight as the blade can stand. Beyond a certain point,

the blade will not spin on command. So go ahead, weight your bodies as needed but always test them for instantaneous spin before you put them to work.

The second most important characteristic of a good spinner is one in which the blade can be felt at all times. This is crucial because it has been proven by myself and countless others that a slow-spinning blade is far more effective than a fast-spinning blade. But the only way in which you know if your blade is spinning slow or fast is if you can feel the individual pulsations of the blade on your rod tip. Blade feel is caused by the centrifugal force of the blade every time it turns around the shaft. This pulsation is then transmitted to the line and then to the rod tip. It is through these pulsations that you can learn to control the spinner for slow-blade spin as outlined in the following chapters.

Slow-blade spin is most critical in sizes #3 and up. (In sizes #2 and below, we don't concern ourselves with it.) If you pull on a blade, size #3 and up, and you have no tap-tap-tap feel on your rod tip, *even if the blade spins instantaneously,* this is no good. Your success will decrease for two important reasons: First, if you cannot feel the blade, you

The spinner on the right is center-balanced by reversing the last two beads or using a body that is heaviest in the middle. It makes for a better spinner that will spin better and sink better.

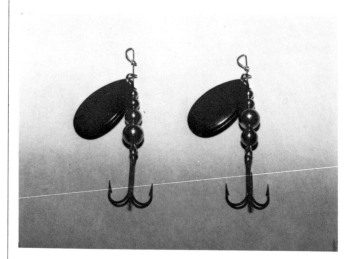

cannot control for the slow-blade spin which is more effective than a fast-blade spin. Second, a blade that is smooth and has no tap-tap-tap on the rod tip is not sending vibrations through the water. *It therefore can only attract through vision but not through sound.* Thus, the radius from which you can attract is significantly reduced. A blade that is smooth and does not send pulsations to the rod tip is a *dead blade.* It has not been tuned by the manufacturer. Stay away from it!

Shaft

I like to use spinner shafts with a preformed eye for the hook. This is because spinners can be made much more quickly. The hook is placed on the preformed eye. Then the body is slipped over both ends of the wire. This, in turn, locks the hook onto the shaft. Suggestions are given below for the gauge wire to be used with each size spinner.

Suggested Guidelines for Making Weighted Steelhead Spinners with French Blades				
Blade Size	Clevis Size	Hook Size	Wire Shaft Diameter	Body Length
0	1	10	.030	11mm
1	1	10,8	.030	13mm
2	2	6	.030	17mm
3	2	6,4	.030	21mm
4	2	4	.030	26mm
5	2	2	.030	34mm

Hooks

In his fine book *Steelhead Drift Fishing*, author Bill Luch cites a study conducted which compared the hooking effectiveness of single versus treble hooks. The conclusion drawn was that single hooks are just as effective as trebles in hooking fish. I disagree. When the proper style and size treble is used, the treble stands out as being considerably more effective. This opinion is supported by tackle manufacturers themselves. Few commercially-produced spinners come with a single hook. If single hooks were comparable, they would be used in lieu of trebles because it would help cut manufacturing costs. There is another thing I don't like about single siwash-style hooks. Because the hook shank is longer, the fish generally takes the hook deeper in an effort to reach the lure. I have mangled a greater percentage of fish with these hooks than I have with trebles. Because I like to release most of my steelhead, I want to hook my fish in the shallow portion of the mouth.

All treble hooks are not alike. Many anglers feel there is little difference and buy the cheapest available or buy the improper style. This mistake will catch up with them very quickly. On commercially-made spinners, it is common to see improper style. In addition, manufacturers often go one size smaller than is needed in an effort to cut costs. The finest hooks for steelhead are round-bend trebles. The V.M.C. 9649 is an excellent hook. The Mustad 35647 is also good. This style treble has a shorter shank for fewer missed strikes. The extra-large, wide-bend gap (distance from shank to point) affords greater hooking capacity. The commonly used Mustad 3551 is an excellent quality treble but the short gap will result in missed strikes.

Please note that choice of treble on No. 5 spinners may be limited by state regulations. A No. 2 round-bend is illegal in Michigan because regulations specify how large the gap can be on a treble. For example, one Michigan angler uses the V.M.C. 9617 in place of the 9649 on his No. 5 spinners. He reports satisfactory results.

Shank Tubing

Tubing on the hook shank is strictly an adornment and has got nothing to do with function. However, yellow, red, orange, and green tubing is such a standard item on sizes 3, 4 and 5 spinners that many consider it to be an essential item. Tubing has two purposes. First it adds color and gaudiness to the spinner which is desirable in various circumstances. This helps with the spinner's ability to attract a

steelhead's attention. Second, bright tubing helps direct the strike of the fish to the hook. This increases chances for a solid hook-up. Rarely do I ever experience a take from the side or a lateral take on a winter steelhead and all my winter steelhead spinners have tubing on the shank. Spoons generally do not have shank tubing and lateral takes are much more common. On my smaller sizes 1 and 2 summer steelhead spinners, I do not use tubing because too much size, color, or flash will spook the steelhead. Interestingly, I do get some lateral takes. In short, I highly recommend shank tubing for winter steelhead spinners. For summer steelhead, use of tubing will depend on the size spinner used and the conditions fished. This will be discussed in a later chapter.

Lure Tape

This, again, is pretty much a standard item on all blades except when using tiny spinners or a black blade. Tape does not influence function except when applied in a very sloppy or nonsymmetrical manner.

The Osborne No. 155 Revolving Punch is excellent for punching out dots on pressure-sensitive tapes. You would need to order this from a good hardware store.

A strip of lure tape is vertically applied to the middle of one side of the blade to add color and gaudiness to the spinner. Orange, fire orange, chartreuse, hot pink, and kelly green are the most commonly used colors. The key to the tape's effectiveness is realized by applying the tape on the *inside* of the blade. I will explain why. Toss out a spinner with tape applied in this fashion. As you reel in, the tape will be barely visible. But as you reel it past you and you start to view the spinner laterally and from the rear, the lure tape will become visible and, in essence, the lure will look as if it changed in appearance. Oftentimes, a steelhead catches a lateral glimpse of a spinner as it is quartered downstream. At some point in our drift, the spinner will catch the current and will change direction. A change in lure direction excites steelhead for some unknown reason and it is common knowledge that a fish often strikes as soon as a fly or lure swings in the current. If the fish has been chasing the lure from a lateral viewpoint and, all of a sudden, he now sees something a little different from a rear view, this change in appearance is a further exciter and will increase the chances of inducing the fish into striking.

While this principle works in reverse by applying tape to the outside of the blade, it is not as effective. I personally like to have the outside of my blade free of tape so that it realizes its full flash-producing potential. This is especially true when using silver-plated blades. By placing tape on the outside, I add color but at the expense of reducing metallic flash. As the inside of the blade rotates around body and shaft, the view of its flash is somewhat impeded by the body which blocks it out.

Miscellaneous Adornments

Anyone who has ever looked at a mail-order catalog that sells lure parts will see dozens of different-sized round- and oval-shaped beads offered in many different colors. While such adornments may provide visual appeal on the store shelf or take up unused room on the spinner shaft, I do not think they add to the fish-catching effectiveness of steelhead spinners. They have relatively little weight and using them in place of a solid metal body decreases weight which in most cases is undesirable. While they do add color, they are not nearly as bright as fluorescent tape or tubing. Most importantly, they have no purpose as was explained for tape and tubing. My opinion: Use of an adornment or lure part just for the sake of using it or just because it "looks good" is no justification for using it. Every part of your spinner should have a specific purpose.

There is one specific use of colored beads that you may want to try. You will notice that on many summer steelhead flies a different colored butt section is used on the body. This provides the same effect as does lure tape when applied to the inside of the blade. As it swings in the current, the fly's visual appearance changes which in turn acts as an exciter and further induces strikes. I have used this technique when using black bodies. A tiny yellow, red, or orange bead is placed at the rear. It can be very effective!

Color Coordination — Tape and Tubing

When fishing spinners, I like to use only one color tape and tubing with my spinners. I will be the first to admit that different color combinations placed on the blade and body can be very effective. But then I ask, "Was it the chartreuse or the red that attracted the fish most?" Adding extra variables complicates my quest for determining those factors that made the lure effective. As a result of this dilemma, I use only one color on any one spinner. And, if I add orange to the blade and hook shank, I make sure that both colors are closely matched. By practicing the latter, I can be sure which color is causing the lure to be effective.

My early experience in Oregon demonstrates the point. When we moved to Eugene, I did not know anyone who seriously fished spinners for steelhead so I was on my own to figure out effective combinations. During the summer, I discovered that silver-plated spinners adorned with chartreuse were effective on summer-runs when fished under cloudy skies. As I continued to fish into the fall, my success plummeted after November 15th. Having no experience with Oregon winter steelhead, I attributed my lack of success to other factors. I continued to fish silver and chartreuse until one day in late January. After throwing spinners all day in what looked to be magnificent water, I switched to silver and fire orange and immediately hooked a cutthroat. Later on, my partner momentarily hooked a steelhead on a silver and orange spoon. From that point on, I used silver and orange and started making consistent catches. In fact, to this day, I use little else besides this combination of orange and silver for winter steelhead. Had I originally adorned my spinner with two or three different colors, I probably would have been confused as to which color made the lure most effective. This is why, initially, I recommend using one color of adornment with your spinners. Through experimentation, this simple practice will help you to much more quickly determine which colors are proving to be effective. Unless you have considerable experience with steelhead spinner fishing, multiple colors will confuse and may also retard your progress.

Color Coordination — Body

This is a bit more tricky. I do not necessarily recommend using one metallic finish unless you are looking for maximum or minimum flash and visibility. On the color plate, you will notice two summer steelhead spinners — McKenzie Medium and McKenzie Dark. On the former, a purposely-tarnished brass body is used. In this case, I wanted to use a toned-down spinner but was not interested in reducing flash and brightness to a minimum. The brass adds a bit of highlight when used in conjunction with a brass blade. On the McKenzie Dark, a totally toned-down spinner was desired. In this case, I went with black blade and tarnished brass body. The McKenzie Dark is a case in which a combination of two finishes are used to create an overall degree of flash.

On the opposite extreme, we have the winter steelhead spinners. If the goal is to maximize flash, use of the brightest metallic-finished body with a silver-plated blade is desirable. This is why I silver-plate the whole thing.

General Dimensions and Precautions

The chart on page 23 is a suggested guide for building spinners with the various-sized French-type blades. Staying within these guidelines will insure a properly designed spinner. The only thing this chapter does not cover is body weight. Be careful. A one-ounce lead worm weight used for a 26mm No. 4 is not going to function properly. You will have trouble getting the blade to start and the spinner blade won't rotate at slow speeds. If you wish to find a weight limit, you will have to experiment. I have never felt a need to build the heaviest spinner possible. My No. 5s weigh slightly more than a half-ounce, and my No. 4s weigh slightly more than a third of an ounce. Below No. 4, one is really talking about summer steelhead spinners. Clear, shallow waters make weighting less of a concern although casting distance is still a consideration on the larger rivers. I weight my small summer steelhead spinners only enough to achieve the desired casting range.

A few precautions should be taken in building spinners. Never leave enough empty space between clevis and eye so that the body can move up the spinner shaft thereby exposing the short end of the wire on the preformed spinner shaft.

Both ends of the spinner shaft fit into the hole in the body. This anchors the hook in the preformed eye. If one end is exposed, a fish will immediately straighten out the preformed eye and the hook will release. You will be left with a spinner minus the hook and fish. It is all right if the body can be moved up the shaft toward the front of the spinner, just as long as both ends of the shaft remain securely anchored inside the hole of the body.

During the course of fishing, the body may move up the spinner shaft just a bit. This causes the hook to wobble and the body to shake. This in turn causes extra resistance and impedes performance. When you see this phenomenon occurring, simply slip the body to the rear of the spinner.

Never sandwich the clevis so closely that it touches both the bearing and the front eye of the spinner. Always make sure that a little room is left so that the clevis is free to move and that when spinning, it touches *only* the bearing to the rear.

I have seen spinners with a small colored bead or two placed *ahead* of the clevis. This is done for human eye appeal and is a perfect example of useless, nonfunctional cosmetics. Such gimmicks and trinkets add nothing to the lure but do add friction to the clevis which will decrease blade responsiveness.

Swivels

Before finishing the spinner, you may want to consider permanently installing a barrel swivel in the eye of the spinner. The reason for use of any swivel is to avoid line twist caused by a constantly rotating body. Anglers typically tie a snap-swivel to the end of their line and then snap the terminal end to their lure. My objections to this arrangement number two: first, any time you add swivels to your rig, the true feel of your lure becomes obscured. The more you add, the more obscured the feel becomes. We want to create an arrangement in which the least amount of snaps and swivels are used.

Second, most swivels are large in size relative to the size of the spinner. By adding a snap-swivel, the swivel then becomes part of the lure and you end up with a lure larger than was intended. My solution has been to install a No. 12 barrel swivel directly into the eye of the spinner on sizes 3, 4, and 5. By going this route, the snap is eliminated, thereby leaving a tiny swivel on the eye that does not obscure feel and does not appreciably influence the overall size of the spinner. I use No. 12 black Romer barrel swivels. Black seems to work better than the plain brass as in the water it gives the suggestion of a creature's eye. Also, by being black, it is less prone to catch the fish's attention.

On smaller sizes 0, 1, and 2 spinners I do not finish the eye with a swivel. Instead, I use a 10- to 18-inch leader between spinner and a No. 12 black barrel swivel. On occasion, small trout will peck at the swivel but, overall, I have found these incidents to be more amusing than hindering.

Finishing the Eye

Finishing the eye can be done in one of two ways. The photo shows the various steps of finishing the spinner by hand with needle-nose pliers. A wire former can be used in lieu of the latter. Most mail-order houses offer wire formers of some kind. Whichever way you finish your spinner is strictly a matter of personal preference. The wire former is

safer and easier. Use of pliers is quicker and a bit more exact. I used to use a wire former when working with .030 gauge wire. When working with .024 gauge, I have always

The different stages of finishing a spinner using needle-nose pliers. Spinner should stay within the grasp of pliers until the very last stage of cutting off excess. It takes a little practice.

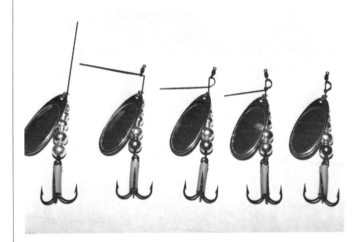

used pliers. Whatever you use, be sure to leave at least a 1/16-in. space between clevis and eye. I leave 1/8- to 1/4-in. to compensate for movement of the body up the shaft. My general advice is that too much room is better than too little room. Caution should be used not to leave more than 1/4-in., the reason being that too large a space sometimes causes the spinner to wobble due to lack of stabilization in the empty space on the shaft.

Buying Spinners

Although good commercially-produced spinners are available, I personally was never able to find exactly what I was looking for. I often regard the purchase of commercially-produced spinners as being a trade-off. One brand is weighted properly but has a .018-in. blade. Another has the silver blade you were looking for but the body is not fully weighted and the improper style and size hook is used. If you prefer to buy, the best approach is to prioritize the various features for a given use and then try to find as many of the features you have listed starting with the first one or two.

There are a few qualities of steelhead spinners that are, in general, desirable at all times. Using a spinner with a French-type blade is the number one priority. Colors, weighting, hook style, and tubing are meaningless unless that blade is turning. The French-type blade turns at all speeds. The second consideration should be weighting. Steelhead are bottom-hugging fish and French-type blades cause considerable resistance. Sufficient weight is needed to keep that spinner down. The third consideration should be hook size and style. Most of the quality spinners available today employ round-bend trebles. These hooks give a solid hook-up. Insist on buying spinners with these hooks. A good strike from a steelhead is too precious of a thing to be lost as a result of bad hooks. Good hooks are not cheap. Cheap hooks are not good.

Rather than review ready-made spinners here, I will make suggestions as I discuss strategy in later chapters. In this way, the discussion of any one particular spinner will then seem more relevant and be more meaningful.

Where to Buy Spinner Parts

Should you decide to seriously pursue spinner fishing, you will no doubt want to start building your own spinners. This means that most everything you will need will be bought mail-order, the reason being that making home-made spinners is a very specialized craft (although this is changing). As a result, there are not that many retail outlets that carry a wide variety of components.

When it comes to getting spinner components, the interested angler will find that they are easily obtainable. With regard to these components, I have chosen to list only those firms that 1) I have personally dealt with, 2) provided good service and reasonable pricing. While other suppliers, no doubt, exist, I do not want to risk my credibility by recommending a retailer that I never checked out. There have been specific instances in which I have been misrepresented by suppliers claiming that "these are what Jed Davis uses." For example, I never advised or never would advise 1) the use of *black nickel* finishes on blades or bodies or 2) the substitution of lime green or forest green tape for genuine Kelly green, the latter which is commonly used on the *Summer Green* spinner. (See Chapter on summer steelhead.)

My own company, Pen Tac, has been supplying spinner components to steelhead, salmon and trout anglers since 1991. Even though it is my company and I stand to profit from sales, I have to single it out because my partner and I have spent 7 years with a concerted effort to manufacture, from scratch, components that are specifically designed for the steelhead, salmon and trout angler. In any event, anyone interested in building their own spinners should acquaint themselves with a variety of components from the firms listed below. They will all work for you. If they didn't work, I wouldn't list them.

In this regard, it might be helpful to mention that 100 expert spinner anglers will all fish a little differently. I, naturally, have preferences for certain blades, bodies, etc. But this does not mean that there are other ways of doing it. The point is this: When selecting spinner components, use what feels right and use those components which you have the most confidence in.

Manufacturers / Distributors

Lakeland Tackle
Isle, Minnesota 56342
These folks supply mail-order houses and retailers with many of their components as listed above. If you have a business, you may be able to get their catalog.

Worth Mfg.
Stevens Point, Wisconsin 54481
This firm also supplies the traditional-type components to mail-order houses such as Hille, Netcraft, Reed, etc. If you have a business, you may be able to get their catalog.

This sportsman's case from Bass Pro Shops is great for carrying and protecting spinners. The case floats and the foam absorbs excess moisture from wet spinners.

Mail-Order Houses

Pen Tac Corporation
Spinner Components Division
P.O. Box 18273
Seattle, Washington 98118   (206) 722-1700
This is Jed Davis's firm that began offering spinner and spoon components in September, 1991. A catalog is available and Jed personally helps out first-time customers or novices with spinner selection for the particular rivers they fish.

Netcraft
2800 Tremainsville Road
Toledo, Ohio 43613
Netcraft is primarily oriented to the spin fisherman although they do carry a little of everything. You can get some of the traditional components that spinner makers have been using for many years. It is fun just to look through the Netcraft catalog. A lot of unusual items. Write for a catalog.

E. Hille
P.O. Box 996
Williamsport, Pennsylvania 17703
Hille is oriented to mainly fly anglers but they also carry the traditional components. Write for catalog.

Cabela's
812-13th Avenue
Sidney, Nebraska 69160
Right after we got married, Lori and I headed west from New York City. Several nights later, we were forced to exit in western Nebraska because we needed gas. The small town which we were in did not have a single gas station open. We fell asleep in the car and when we awoke, we were sitting right in front of Cabela's, a place I have ordered a lot of fishing gear from. They have a large color catalog with a lot of traditional-type components. Be careful about buying these French blades. As of this writing, their standard blade was .018" which is unacceptable but they did offer a .0247". If you buy from them, make sure you get the latter.

Chapter 4

Silver Plating and Black Oxide

WHEN I SPEAK WITH FELLOW ANGLERS ABOUT my spinner technique, the issue of silver plating and, to a lesser extent, black oxide plating always seems to pop up at some point in the conversation. As relatively few anglers plate their spinners, there seems to be a tendency for these sportsmen, new to steelhead spinner fishing, to believe that silver and black oxide are "the secrets" that will increase their luck by leaps and bounds. Now it is true that I depend heavily upon silver and black oxide but only under specific circumstances that I will discuss in a later chapter. Consistently successful steelhead spinner fishing is much like fly fishing in that it is an intellectual game where the right size and finish lure must be matched to the prevailing environmental conditions. Large silver-plated blades are worthless for 75 percent of all summer steelhead conditions. On the other hand, use of a black blade for winter steelheading will severely limit one's catch under many conditions.

The point I wish to make is that neither silver nor black oxide is the "end-all" answer to steelhead spinner fishing. Oftentimes, I have seen anglers get carried away with the idea of silver plating to the point that they will not fish anything but silver-plated blades. Such a mistake will lead to erratic catches because terminal tackle will only be matched to one set of environmental circumstances. Nevertheless, anyone interested in pursuing the spinner technique should seriously consider plating blades. As we shall see, silver and black oxide each possess desirable qualities that under the right conditions can do a real number on steelhead!

One of the problems with obtaining desirable finishes for our spinner blades and bodies is that, of this writing, no retail supplier of spinner parts offers silver or black oxide blades. Only nickel, brass, copper, and sometimes gold finishes are available. There are three reasons for the absence of silver and black oxide. First, is the expense. Silver is a precious metal. The retail price of the blade would have to be doubled and this would put a lot of people off. Black oxide blades must be racked by hand for plating. The time and labor involved in obtaining the finish also puts a large price tag on the finished blade. Second, most anglers simply do not understand why genuine silver or black oxide may be desirable in terms of fish-catching ability.

In fact, I would venture to say that in the case of silver, most anglers don't even know when they are buying a silver-plated blade! All they know is that this model "works." The third reason is related to silver only: If you take silver- and nickel-plated blades and put them side by side, the difference between the two in most lighting situations is subtle. The average guy looks at both and says, "They are both shiny and "silver" colored. Why should I pay twice the price for genuine silver?"

For these reasons, we are then forced to plate our own blades or have a plating house do it for us. This means time and money. As no tackle supplier that I know of offers silver-plating kits, the price to get started is around $40.00 or $50.00. I have gotten a lot of letters and phone calls from anglers anxious to do their own plating only to find out that in order to get started they had to put out a sizable chunk of money. While one batch of silver-plating solution will plate 3,000 blades and parts, anglers are reluctant to make the investment when all they really wanted was three dozen blades to try out. Any major city such as Portland, Seattle, Detroit, or Milwaukee has a number of plating houses which will be happy to plate blades and brass bodies. In general, however, they only like to plate large quantities. This may be desirable for the experienced spinner fisherman who has got his technique down and who goes through several hundred spinners a year, but not for the curious angler who is getting started.

I suggest that newcomers to the spinner technique stick

to nickel, brass, and copper initially. While there may be some limitations, the angler (who is otherwise designing his spinners properly and fishing them in an effective manner) can make excellent catches year-round. Silver and black oxide do add advantage and versatility to one's arsenal but unless the other important components are present, these two finishes will represent nothing more than a worthless indulgence.

The Lure of Silver

The most popular season for steelhead fishing is late fall, winter, and spring. Whether fishing an Oregon coastal stream or a Lake Michigan tributary, three factors remain constant: increased water flow; cold water; and, many times, off-colored water. Colder water means that steelhead metabolism will be below its peak. This in turn means that we will have to present something that excites the fish to such a degree that they will strike a lure in spite of low metabolism. Off-colored water limits visibility under water. It is therefore essential to present the brightest and flashiest-finished lure to insure that the spinner's image is seen over the longest distances. Increased water flow means that the stream becomes deeper and wider. A larger river has many more holding areas. The fish are more scattered over a wider range. To get the attention of steelhead, we want to present a bait that can be seen over the greatest radius.

A genuine silver-finished blade accomplishes the above better than any finish. Compared to nickel or brass, it is brighter and lighter. Unlike the others, its mirror-like finish reflects most of the light that hits it. The result is a bright, strobe light-like flash that excites and gives the spinner visibility greater than what can be attained with any of the other conventional finishes. This is precisely why it is such a valuable tool.

Confusing Nickel and Silver

A lot of fishermen put a silver and nickel blade side by side under strong light and conclude that there is little difference between the amount of light each reflects. True, both will reflect light quite well under these conditions. But this is not how steelhead are exposed to the blade. The photo (on page 31) of two blades placed side by side simulates what actually does occur under water when filtered light hits the blade. The nickel blade, on the left, gives off a much darker flash than does the silver-plated blade. Because silver is lighter, it better reflects light that hits it. While nickel is silver-like in appearance, it is relatively darker and absorbs a much higher percentage of the light. This translates into a dull, darker flash.

Part of the confusion over nickel and silver has to do with the shininess versus lightness dichotomy. Any polished metallic surface can be made to shine. This adds brilliance, sparkle, and luster to the surface. Using shininess as a criterion, silver and nickel blades appear to be equally bright. In reality, it is *lightness* that determines the blade's reflectivity or flash capacity. Silver is lighter than nickel. That's why it is the preferred finish for high, off-colored water.

How Much Better Is Silver?

I would venture to estimate that spinners are up to 25 percent more effective if a silver finish is employed in cold, high, or off-colored water flows. Putting it another way,

in three out of four situations, it probably would not matter which finish was employed. That is, a steelhead would hit a nickel just as well as a silver. There are borderline or *threshold* situations that do set silver apart from nickel. For example, at 39°F., a steelhead is going to have a low metabolism. The added flash of silver may trigger the strike of a fish that is some distance from the spinner.

I will say this: I would bet my money on the angler fishing nickel but who otherwise is fishing effectively versus the man fishing silver who is a bit green on technique. Silver-plated spinners for *winter steelhead* can be darn good . . . but only if you have got the goods to go along with them.

The Silver-Plating Process

The plating process is relatively simple. After one or two plating sessions, you will have the technique mastered. But there are things that can go wrong if you do not follow the procedure carefully.

The first concern is your health and safety. The silver-plating solution is composed of three chemicals, two of which are highly poisonous. Keep the solution in a safe place, away from children, pets, food, and cooking utensils. In addition, should the solution come into contact with acid, a poisonous cyanide gas will be be released. It is unlikely that you will have acid lying around, but keep this in mind. Make sure that you plate in a well-ventilated area. Open the window or turn on the fan if plating in a bathroom. Make sure there are no cuts on your hands; if there are, wear a pair of thin surgical gloves or wait until the wound heals completely. Finally, all utensils to be used should be cleaned thoroughly before and after use. Contact with an undesirable element may cause a harmful chemical reaction.

You will need three chemicals which, depending on where you live, may be somewhat difficult to obtain. To mix one batch for plating, you will need one-half ounce of silver nitrate, one-half ounce of sodium cyanide, and one ounce of sodium carbonate. Silver nitrate can sometimes be obtained from a pharmacy. Sodium carbonate is harmless and can be obtained at a hobby store. Sodium cyanide will either have to be obtained from a chemical supply house or through a hobby shop that specializes in stocking chemicals. Sodium carbonate is relatively cheap. Silver nitrate is expensive, costing $15.00 to $20.00 per one-half ounce. This price fluctuates with the market value of pure silver. Sodium cyanide cannot be obtained in small quantities because of lack of demand. Therefore, one generally has to purchase one pound — a life supply — for around $20.00. The payoff is that one batch prepared with these amounts will plate 3,000 blades or parts. This comes out to one-and-a-half cents per part. Even if you are a spinner spinner fanatic like me, one batch of plating solution will last several years.

Take all three chemicals and place them in a *glass* jar or container. Never use anything but glass or glazed ceramic. Add one pint or 470 mm. of *distilled* water. Use of regular water will contaminate the solution. Now mix the solution using either a glass or ceramic mixer. Once again: Use of metal or wood mixers may contaminate the solution. Mixing the solution may take up to 20 minutes. Keep mixing until every bit of the chemicals are dissolved. Most of the chemical granules will mix within the first minute, but a few stubborn nonconformists will hang on to their individuality. Mix them until dissolved!

You will now need a power source. You have two choices: You can buy a 6-volt lantern battery for about $5.00; or you can buy a Shauer, one-amp. battery charger for $15.00 to $20.00. True, the lantern battery is cheaper, but after a couple hours of use it does not give a reliable, consistent current. In addition, it will need to be replaced. In the end, it will end up costing you more money and you will be left with nothing. The one-amp. battery charger will last a lifetime. More importantly, it will yield a consistent charge. This is important for continuously good plating.

A one-amp battery such as this is a reliable power source that won't fade like a regular battery. Note how a simple switch is placed in the circuit so cold-plating and hot-plating may be easily done.

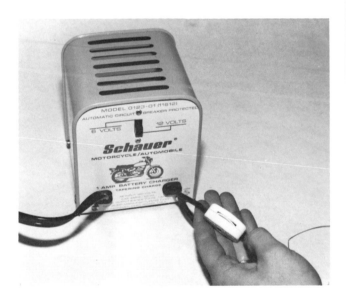

A small hole is drilled through a pure silver coin to which thin copper wire is then easily attached. The copper wire should lead to positive terminal.

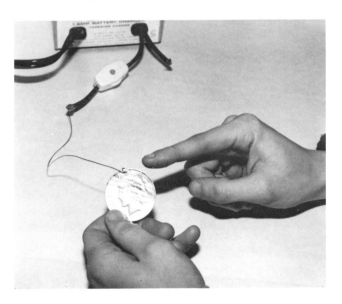

If using the lantern battery, attach a piece of light copper wire to the positive terminal on the battery. Attach the other end of this wire to a piece of genuine silver. If using

A piece of copper wire is attached to the negative terminal and a small hook at the end is made that is used to hold a brass blade or part.

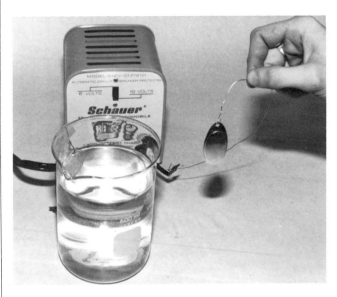

the battery charger, strip the end of the positive wire and attach to the silver. The plating process will slowly erode the silver so do not use jewelry, heirlooms, or anything of personal value. I went to a coin shop and bought the cheapest silver dollar. (Note: Never use sandwich coins; use only a genuine silver piece that is silver throughout.) A half dollar or even a quarter is sufficient, but a silver dollar will allow you to submerge a good portion of the coin into the solution without the potential danger of submerging the wire itself. I drilled a hole at the edge of the coin and placed the copper wire through the hole. This is much better than taping or clipping the copper as the latter is less secure and often falls off. Now partially submerge the silver in the plating solution. Make sure it is secured. Should the wire holding the silver make contact with the solution, you may contaminate the solution. To the negative terminal of the lantern battery or negative wire of the battery charger, attach a piece of light copper wire forming a hook on the very end to hold the blade or brass part.

You will need to take three additional measures. First, when plating a piece, you will need to turn the electrical current on and off while the piece is submerged. This is part of the process. Install a simple switch somewhere in the circuit — anywhere. The only other possibility when using the battery charger is to keep pulling out and putting in the plug; but, when plating large quantities, this will tire you out. Second, when hooking up wires, cut all wires as short as is comfortable to work with. This is because weak 6- and 12-volt currents get diluted when using long excesses of wire. Third, if using the battery charger, set the voltage for 12 volts, not 6 volts. I find that plating works better with 12 volts. You are now ready to plate!

The best plating results will be achieved with *brass* parts. Do not use nickel-plated parts. You will get a very attractive plate, but the silver will not stick. It will start peeling off while fishing. Copper blades also plate well but, because they are more expensive than brass, I would stick with brass blades and parts.

Before outlining the process, two terms need clarification — "cold plating" and "hot plating." Plating with electrical current is referred to as "hot plating." The absence of any electrical current while plating is referred to as "cold plating."

Hang a blade or part on the negative terminal wire. Submerge part and cold plate for five or ten seconds. (Don't worry about the copper wire getting submerged. This is okay.) After waiting five to ten seconds, turn on the electrical current and hot plate for another five to ten seconds. You will notice that the blade will have turned a cloudy gray silver. Remove the blade immediately and wash

"Cold-plate" for a few seconds, then "hot-plate."

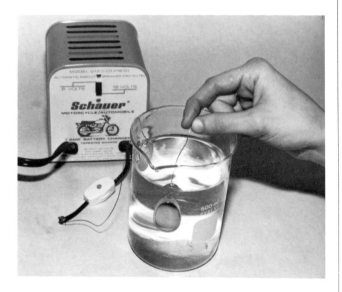

After blade is removed, rinse thoroughly and polish with baking soda and a damp cloth.

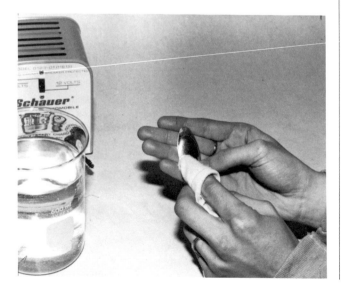

thoroughly with tap water. Now take a damp cloth and with baking soda, polish the blade, rinse, dry, and you now have a genuine silver-plated blade or part.

The result is a genuine silver-plated blade. For situations where maximum flash is necessary, this is the finest finished blade in the world.

The process progresses much faster if you plate the part, rinse, and then put all the plated pieces in a jar of water to be polished when you finish plating.

It is important to note that, initially, you might probably waste a number of blades or parts. As blades are polished, the silver might peel off. Do not get alarmed! A new solution is sometimes almost too strong and it takes about 10 to 20 blades before its starts working well. If the problem persists, add 10 ml. of distilled water to the solution and mix well. However, once the solution starts working well, it will work until you use it all up.

The amount of time that you cold and hot plate will vary from part to part and even from one solution to the next. This variable is directly related to surface area of the part. Cycle time for a No. 2 or a No. 3 is less than for a No. 4 or No. 5. If you have been plating No. 5s for two hours and now switch to a No. 2 or to a brass body, experiment with cycle time (i.e., number of seconds you cold plate and hot plate) before plating in quantity. When a desired cycle time is found that produces a satisfactory and durable finish, then begin to plate in quantity.

A bit of advice: When you have found the right combination of cold- and hot-plating time and begin to plate dozens of blades without polishing them, do a spot check every fifteenth blade. Hold up the assembly line and polish a blade just to make sure everything is working well. Occasionally, you may have to readjust cycle time.

After having plated 50 parts, change the light copper wire or cut off the part that is continuously submerged on the negative terminal. You will notice that this wire also gets plated as it is submerged. Buildup from continuous platings dulls the electrical contact with the blade so it is a good idea to change it.

The plating solution, when not in use, will last indefinitely if covered in an airtight container and stored in a cool, *dark* place. Because one batch of solution will plate approximately 3,000 blades or parts, it will be possible to use the same solution for many, many years.

Shiny Blades Versus Light Blades

When silver plating, it is possible to adjust the silver finish. A quick hot-plating time with cold-plating will yield a very shiny blade but only slightly lighter than nickel. A slow hot-plating time without cold-plating will yield a very light white finished blade markedly lighter than nickel but it will be more of a dull, matted finish. It is a sacrifice of one for the other. You cannot get the best of both. I generally opt for the more matted finish but not to the point where all gloss is lost. For comparison, a Rooster Tail blade employs a light, matted finish. A Mepps blade is more shiny but less light.

The Lure of Black

The greatest amount of flash can be obtained by using a silver blade. Why then would we ever consider the use of a blade that gives off the least amount of flash? There are three reasons. First, steelhead can become very nervous and skittish in water 52° and above. They are easily spooked by shadows, sounds, and especially by offerings that are too big or flashy. Because a typical spinner offers considerable visual and sonic attraction, steelhead may ignore it or be spooked. In water flows that exceed 52°, water levels will generally be lower and the water will often be gin clear. This, coupled with other factors, may render the threshold of attraction to be very low. Stated another way, the amount of flash and visibility needed to excite and arouse curiosity may be much lower. Our goal is to excite but not spook. A black blade can do just that. It offers presence without being too threatening. The most typical use of a black blade is for summer steelhead on a hot day in bright sunlight on a shallow riffle. To the surprise of many steelheaders, these fish are often quite eager to strike, but only if one's offering is small, dark, and even dull.

The second reason for black has to do with feeding. Some steelhead, especially fall summer-runs, will feed, although feeding habits tend to be somewhat opportunistic, casual, and erratic. Perhaps a struggling caddis or a drowned beetle drifts directly in the fish's path. A steelhead may be inclined to pick it up. Whatever it is, most of what a steelhead eats in the river is dark or black. Should one encounter a feeding steelhead, a black blade can be a very effective tool. I will never forget one fall several years ago on Oregon's North Umpqua. After a thrilling battle with one of the river's famed summer-runs, I hefted the large fish from the water to find a spinner embedded deep in the fish's throat. This happened repeatedly. Only a fish interested in eating would ever take a bait like that.

The third reason for black blades is partially related to the second reason. Black, in itself, is a very attractive color to steelhead. This probably relates to the fact that as fingerlings and smolts, much of the young steelhead's diet consisted of small dark insects, snails, and scuds. With such a history, black may trigger a learned response from the past.

Black Oxide

As elaborated upon above, the black blade is very effective for summer-runs in various conditions. Why then

don't I paint my blades? The reason is simple. Paint applied to metals is very prone to chipping. If steelhead were to be found in the weed beds of lakes or in the back sloughs of the Columbia River, then chipping would not be a concern. However, fishing on the bottom over gravel and sharp rocks is like putting a blade in a food disposal. The finish chips or peels quickly. The only solution is to electronically plate metal blades such that the finish becomes part of the metal. This can be achieved with black oxide. The black oxide finish on a blade will eventually begin to wear off but intolerable levels of wear generally exceed the life of the spinner. It is not a concern.

The lighter, brighter blade is silver-plated. The other, a common nickel-plated blade. This photo simulates what is seen under water. Placing two blades under a light bulb does not give an accurate appraisal of underwater flash. Jed Davis photo

Like with silver, quality black oxide blades are difficult to find. In fact, the only French-type chromes that I know of are on the Mepps Black Fury, Vibrax, and Panther Martin. Prior to having my own blades plated by a plating house, I would buy Black Furies. I would then dismantle the spinner, take the blade and discard the rest. I was forced to pay $2.59 every time I needed a black blade—a very expensive way to fish!

My original solution to this problem had been to take large quantities of brass blades and parts to plating firms. Because these firms plate for manufacturers who contract for thousands of parts at a time, they would often see us individuals as somewhat of a nuisance. But, a little bit of persistence got the job done and I had an almost lifetime supply.

When Pen Tac opened its spinner components division in 1989, high quality silver and black oxide blades became available for the first time. Since we do all our own plating, we were able to attain the precise finishes, which through experience, proved to be most effective.

Chapter 5

How to Fish the Spinner

AS WAS OUR YEARLY CUSTOM, MY DAD AND I travelled to Canada every summer during my childhood and young adult years to fish for bass, trout, walleyes, and pike. During the summers of 1965 and 1966, we fished the Rideau Lake System near Kingston, Ontario. Although our efforts produced some good fishing, neither our party nor anyone else's could ever match the catches of a guide by the name of Carl White. Regardless of conditions or time of the year, he always got good numbers of fish for his clients. No wonder he was booked years in advance! Finally, my Dad and I had an opportunity to guide with him for a precious two days. We watched him like a hawk as he systematically derived the proper formula for success. He never failed. He knew his fish, what they liked, and in what conditions they liked it. Having no idea that some day my career would center around sport fishing, it occurred to me as I watched Carl that if I ever wanted to become a consistently successful angler, I was going to have to learn to fish scientifically or systematically. Although Carl White fished for different species on different types of water systems, his approach to fishing is similar to the one elaborated upon here.

The purpose of the next two chapters is to give you a general framework for how to effectively fish a steelhead stream using spinners, such that you are able to consistently catch steelhead. This includes an explanation of what type of water to look for, how the spinner should be presented, and what environmental factors the angler should keep close tabs on while on the river. After hundreds of hooked steelhead, I can confidently state that should you discipline yourself to fish in the manner suggested, you will not only eliminate the guesswork from steelheading but you will also eventually start catching steelhead with a consistency you may have thought not to be possible in this day and age.

But I also want to stress that getting to this point takes concentration, dedication, lots of experience, and hard work, especially if you never approached your fishing this way. As I said in the beginning of this book, I do not find it at all difficult to hook steelhead on spinners but did I ever pay the price to get to this point.

Polarized Sunglasses

The value of always wearing polarized sunglasses, except at dawn and dusk, cannot be overemphasized. Polarized elements in the lenses block out rays that cause surface glare on the water. This affords the angler the opportunity to see well below the water's surface. While identification of potential holding water is made easier, added underwater vision helps identify waters where fish never hold. Let me point out an example. There is one section of Oregon's Siuslaw that is very choppy when waters reach their winter levels. Although the water is only two- to three-feet deep, the turbulence plus the fact that the river never runs gin-clear in the winter, causes the angler to be fooled into thinking that this may be good steelhead holding water. Put on a pair of polarized sunglasses and you will find out differently.

Polarized sunglasses are of added value even when good water has already been identified. I am thinking of a miniature lie on the South Umpqua River that always gives me a couple of steelhead per season. For a few years, this miniature pool had a three-foot branch submerged at its head at a depth of about four feet. One's first inclination would be to toss the lure to the head of the pool, let it sink, and retrieve slowly. Should this be tried, a snag would most surely result and trying to free the lure may spook available fish. With polarized sunglasses, I was always able to reacquaint myself with this snag and thereby avoid it. However, it was nearly impossible to identify this snag without the use of polarized sunglasses.

The above examples are meant to show how one is at a considerable disadvantage when *not* using polarized sunglasses. I feel their use to be so important that if I got up in the morning and discovered I had lost my pair, I would forget about fishing for the day unless I could buy a pair in a reasonable amount of time. For this reason, I keep a spare pair in my drift boat.

If you read the various fishing magazines, you have no doubt seen advertisements for various specially-designed fisherman's sunglasses. Many of these are polarized, but are overpriced and offer no advantages over drugstore models. It is pointless to spend $25.00 for a pair of mail-order glasses when you can find a pair equally as good at a drugstore for $7.00 to $12.00. Almost all pairs that are polarized will say so on the label. Sometimes labels get misplaced or switched. To be sure your pair is polarized, a simple foolproof experiment can be performed right in the store. Place two lenses of two pairs of what you think are polarized sunglasses adjacent to one another. Now turn one pair clockwise or counterclockwise as you look through both lenses against a lighted background. At one point, the view through the lenses should be very clear but, as you turn, it should become increasingly dark, eventually blocking out all light. If one of the two pairs is not polarized, the combination of both lenses will never darken regardless of how you turn the lenses.

Spinner Water

A lot of sportsmen assume that when fishing spinners, the angler covers the same water that is covered by the drift fisherman who searches the bottom with pencil lead and eggs or bobber. This is probably the single biggest mistake made by drift fishermen attempting to use spinners. Not all of the steelhead I catch come from classic drift water. In fact, fewer than 45% of all the steelhead I catch come from classic drift water. To fish spinners effectively, you have got to learn to see a river in a way that is often different from how a drift fisherman sees the river. What's more, there are certain drifts that may be very appealing to the drifter but not to the spinner angler and vice versa. Why the disparity between two techniques, if both sets of anglers are going after the same fish with the same habits? The answer is that both general classes of terminal tackle have limitations that prevent their optimal use in certain types of water.

Any size spinner is limited in the amount of weight it can carry. A too-heavily-weighted spinner will not spin. The spinner is ineffective unless the blade is very responsive and spins freely. With spinners, the preferred French-type blade causes considerable water resistance that forces it to the surface, thereby negating some of the weight. As a result, it is often difficult to fish a fast, deep steelhead slot on a typical winter river due to weight restrictions and resistance problems.

By contrast, drift gear causes very little resistance and the angler is free to use as much weight as is needed to hug the bottom. However, try to drift a three-foot long resting area next to submerged branches or a very slow-moving, three-foot-deep slick where steelhead like to hold when the water temperature is very cold. Try to drift fish an area full of protruding boulders or a tiny undercut bank with roots protruding from shore. Did you ever try to drift fish for

steelhead lying on the edge of fast and slack water or directly behind a small eddy created by a rock? The point I wish to make is that steelhead hold in many different types of water. Each method is more effective than the other in fishing certain types of water. This is why the spinner angler must often ignore what the drift fisherman is fishing and pursue different sections of the drift or find entirely different drifts that are suited to his technique.

A March winter-run makes one last futile attempt to escape the hook. Asa Pearl photo

What characterizes good spinner water? That can be answered in one word: *Definition.* Any river in which the bottom contour can be easily identified is a prime spinner prospect. Spinner sections of rivers have lots of small pockets, pools, riffles, tailouts, protruding boulders, terraces, half-sunken logs, and anything else that, by sight, can be identified as a protective lair. Such rivers tend to be shallow, smaller, snaggier, and slower in speed. It must also be added that various sections of rivers become excellent spinner prospects at various heights. For example, the Wildcat to Richardson's section of Oregon's Siuslaw is an excellent spinner prospect if the water height is at 5.5 feet or below. At 6.5, the height preferred by most drifters and plug pullers, this section is a very poor spinner prospect. I fish a lot of the small forks of major rivers on Oregon's coastal streams. Because drift fishermen make up the vast majority of Northwest steelheaders, you do not see very many anglers on these drifts. The runs are simply too small and snaggy to drift fish and there is not enough room to pull plugs. But for spinner fishing, they are perfect. For the person who fishes the spinner well, these little sparkling jewels can be covered thoroughly and effectively, and often with results that would be hard to match on some of the more popular bumper-to-bumper rivers.

Let's go to the other extreme and talk about poor spinner prospects. Oregon's Alsea is a great producer but, on the rare occasions that I fish it, I don't even bring any spinners with me! The river is small, but it is relatively deep and marked by slot water. The fish tend to congregate in this fast, deep water and are most easily reached by lead and bobber that can be thrown upstream and guided through the various "v"-slots as the rig hugs the bottom. However, it must be pointed out that if the Alsea received a sizeable summer-run, it would be an excellent spinner prospect. At its summer level of 1.3 or 1.9, it becomes very definable.

The rivers that are fast and wide, where most of the fish are taken in runs deeper than eight or ten feet, are usually poor spinner prospects. Put another way, any river in which the angler finds it difficult to consistently fish the bottom of likely holding areas is a poor spinner prospect. Better to leave this water to the drifters. Crowded rivers, where the daily traffic reminds one of the Rose Bowl Parade, are often

The author netting his last Pere Marquette steelhead before moving from Michigan to Oregon in 1981. The "P. M." was his favorite Michigan river. Asa Pearl photo

poor prospects. Steelhead, harassed by dozens of offerings, splashing oars and anchors that transmit continuous sonic booms, will become more timid and much less likely to strike a spinner. Although a less popular river may have a fraction of the fish, you will do much better on a stream like this if you are one of the only anglers fishing.

How to Present a Spinner

Regardless of the conditions you fish, be it an off-colored pool on a winter steelhead stream or a shallow pea-gravelled riffle in gin-clear August water, the spinner is always fished the same way. First and foremost, the angler should strive to fish the lure as close to the bottom as possible. Steelhead are bottom fish and, while both summer and winter strains will travel great distances to strike, they are best enticed under most conditions when presentation is made as close to the bottom as is possible. However, it must be pointed out that inability to reach the bottom because of snag hazards or because the water is very deep should not inhibit you from working these areas. A spinner is an exciter. A steelhead, entranced by its presence or distant flash, will go a long way to strike. This most commonly occurs when fishing the typical Michigan log jam. It is often impossible to cast under large sunken logs where a fish may lie for protection. However, these fish can oftentimes be teased out of their lairs by a spinner that catches their attention some ten feet away. As mentioned above, I generally avoid classic drift water, the type that lies beyond a white-water chute,

because the depth and speed make it difficult to work the spinner deeply. But, there have been a number of times where I hooked fish that rose a considerable distance to take my spinner.

A spinner is most effective when the blade spins at slow to moderate speeds. The slower the blade revolves around the body, the more effective the lure is. Why? This is easily answered by observing a spinner in the water. At a slow speed, it gives off more flash. It gives off a pulsating flash, much like a strobe light or a billboard blinker. At a fast speed, the pulsation and added flash are lost. To me, the difference between a slow-spinning spinner and a fast-spinning spinner is like the difference between looking at a strobe light versus an incandescent light bulb. Interestingly, an incandescent light bulb works on alternating current, but the cycle is so fast that we cannot perceive individual pulsations. If the cycle were considerably reduced, it would be a real attention-getter as are the billboard light bulbs in front of a movie house. Obviously, a blade with more pulsation and flash is a better exciter. That is why working the blade slowly is so desirable. However, it must be pointed out that a slow-spinning blade is not a necessary condition for getting fish to strike. Fast-moving currents in raging winter rivers make it virtually impossible to always fish the lure slowly. Thus, it comes as no surprise that many fish are caught on a fast-spinning blade. In this regard, I will never forget one October morning on the McKenzie River. I made a cast into a very fast riffle directly downstream. The water pressure was so great that the spinner was practically on the surface. I had to adjust something on my boat so I held the rod in one hand, letting the lure hold in the fast current. Then, to my amazement, a steelhead struck hard and solidly. The message here is to work the blade as slowly as possible. However, do not lose confidence if a slow-blade spin cannot be achieved.

At this point a good question may be asked: If the spinner is out of the angler's view, how can one know if the blade is spinning slowly and how does one present the lure to encourage a slow spin? This is one of those sixty-four-dollar questions, the answer which is the very thing that distinguishes the truly good spinner fishermen.

The first part of this answer goes back to the spinner itself. I made a big play for buying a spinner blade that has a .0247-in. thickness as opposed to blades with a .018- or .022-in. thickness. The reason is because the thicker blade is better *felt* while it spins. When a .0247-in. blade is revolving around the shaft at a slow speed, you will feel a tap-tap-tap-tap pulsation on your rod tip. The slower and more deliberate the pulsations, the slower the blade is spinning. If no pulsations are felt, the blade is either not spinning or there is considerable resistance on the blade causing it to spin madly. With a .022-in. blade, pulsations are felt to a lesser degree, and on the .018-in. blade, there is even less feel, making it difficult to know what the blade is doing. This is why I emphatically recommend spinners with a .0247-in. blade. With a bit of experience, you will fish them much more effectively than the other two blades.

Before continuing, a few words must be said about pulsations. The larger the spinner, the easier the pulsating tap-tap will be felt on the rod tip. On well-constructed No. 3, 4 and 5 spinners, you will not have any difficulty in identifying these pulsations. On a No. 2, you will notice a big difference when compared to the larger spinners. Pulsations will be less distinct and faster. To counter this change, I almost always use a shorter, lighter, and softer-tipped rod. The change of rod minimizes the difference and I can then, once again, manipulate the spinner blade without seeing it. However, it must be pointed out that the blade on a No. 2 can never be felt as strongly as the blade on a No. 3, 4 or 5. On No. 0 and 1 blades, I don't even worry about a slow-spinning blade, as it is virtually impossible to detect pulsations. In lieu of concentrating on the blade, I try to fish the whole lure as slowly as possible. The use of No. 0 and 1 blades will be very limited. It is much more important to learn how to fish sizes 2 through 5.

The technique of getting the spinner to spin slowly and at the same time working it close to the bottom is the single most difficult aspect of the technique to master. There seems to be an unspoken understanding among steelheaders that to fish a spinner is very easy. All one needs to do is quarter it across and retrieve. How wrong they are! Learning to effectively fish a No. 4 or 5 spinner on a typical winter steelhead river is like learning how to "wake" or "skate" a fly for summer-runs. Having fished every steelhead method, I can say that learning to fish the spinner effectively is one of the more difficult techniques I have learned. And as with any other refined steelhead method, there is simply no substitute for actual river experience. You simply have got to put in the time if it is to be done right. Let's see how it's done.

The first thing you need to do is build or buy a spinner that you feel comfortable with and fish it exclusively until you "know" it. You will master the technique more quickly if you fish one size and weight spinner because you will become familiar with its qualities and soon learn how to manipulate it optimally. Constantly changing to different weights and sizes will impede progress. I recommend starting with winter steelhead and using a No. 4 or 5 spinner with red or orange adornments. With winter steelhead, you can usually get away with using the same type of spinner all season long. Water conditions will usually dictate the use of a No. 4 or 5.

In terms of technique, this is what your learning goal should be: **Most of your fish will come by first, quartering upstream, and, then, as the spinner sinks, putting just enough tension on the line to get the blade to start spinning while at the same time, fishing the lure close to the bottom. Your spinner has to be close to the bottom but cannot touch bottom. Thus, you will have to develop an intuitive feel for how fast your spinner sinks as well as how it works against different types of currents.** Knowing how fast your spinner sinks will determine how much of an angle you will toss the lure upstream. And how do you know if you are doing it correctly? If you feel deliberate tap-tap pulsations on your rod tip and at the same time occasionally bump bottom, then you are fishing 100 percent effectively. The angle at which you throw your spinner will constantly change depending on water depth and speed. In shallow water of three to five feet, throwing a half-ounce spinner upstream at a 45-degree angle will almost always result in a snag. In such a case, you may want to cast 90 degrees to the boat (straight across). In a small, yet deep, scooped-out hole of about ten feet, throwing upstream at a 45-degree

angle and letting the lure sink before retrieval will put you in the right place.

While angle of cast is one important factor, so is the rate of retrieval; i.e., how fast you turn the reel crank. In slow water a faster-line retrieval may be necessary to get the spinner spinning and to keep the lure off the bottom. In fast water, line retrieval may not be necessary at all. In most cases, the rate of line retrieval will be constantly changing. Case in point: the typical cast. The spinner is cast upstream in five feet of water. You let it sink momentarily. You then give a couple of fast cranks to pull up the slack. Pulsations are then felt as the crank is wound very slowly. Midway through the drift, pulsations cease and you begin to hit rocks. Retrieval rate is speeded up until definite pulsations are once again felt. A few seconds later, pulsations have now become too fast so retrieval rate is slowed down. Suddenly, you feel rocks as the pool shallows out. Now you must crank at a moderate pace to avoid snags. The ability to get the spinner working at a slow speed and at the same time having it work near the bottom is referred to as "spinner sense."

It is important to note that the rod tip should be used in conjunction with line retrieval to control tension on the spinner. In many cases, a slight relaxation or increased tension on the rod tip produces the desired result.

A fine buck taken early in the season. Jed Davis photo

Two other important considerations: First, unless your spinner is swinging into an obstruction or undesirable water, always let the spinner swing downstream until it is directly downstream. Then, reel slowly for a few cranks. Many times, steelhead will follow a lure for a long time before striking. Second, it is important, although not imperative, at some point in the drift, to change lure direction. A lot of steelhead will hit a quartered fly or spinner as it swings into the current; i. e., changes direction. Thus, in most cases a deliberate manipulation is not needed. However, should you be fishing in a situation where this will not happen, then try, at some point in the retrieval, to change lure direction. This may cause a semi-reluctant steelhead to strike.

A good spinner fisherman, especially when using No. 4 and 5 spinners, will snag the bottom many times during the course of a day's fishing. If you are fishing a prime 10-foot pool and snag at the best spot in the pool, pat yourself on the back. You're doing it right! Ninety-percent of all snags are freed by a simple manipulation. Unfortunately, most anglers work against themselves by trying to force the spinner by a powerful "macho" yank. Sometimes it works . . . most of the time it does not.

Here's how to do it: Many snags will feel like a strike so instinctively, the angler sets the hook. As soon as you are sure it is not a fish, relax the line and open up your bail for three or four seconds. Now give a good yank. One of two things is likely to have happened which will free the spinner. The weight of the spinner will cause it to fall off the obstruction. A hook tine cannot penetrate rock so it will fall off. If the hook becomes embedded in wood or brush or it is wedged between two rocks, a yank on the line after the bail has been opened and then closed will initially pull the line in the opposite direction due to the resistance of the river current. It will be as if you rowed over to the snag, and got behind it to free the lure. This technique will work 90 percent of the time.

Steelhead Move to Strike!

One of the great myths passed down by a generation of predominantly drift-fishing steelheaders is that winter steelhead will not move very far to strike. For drift fishing, this is true. A steelhead may move laterally two or three feet to meet a bobber, but it's nothing that causes them to move quickly or strike hard. The pickup is usually subtle. However, it is incorrect to assume that this general rule applies to other types of fishing. When fishing spinners, the idea that a winter steelhead will not move very far to strike is cancelled. The fact is that winter steelhead will move great distances to strike a spinner, just like their summer cousins with higher metabolisms. I've seen them chase a spinner twenty feet downstream, follow a spinner right to the boat, or make a fast swirl for a spinner passed three feet above their heads. These occurrences are not unusual or unexpected. Should you make a commitment to steelhead spinner fishing, you will find this out very quickly. The reason they move relates back to our discussion in Chapter 1. A spinner *excites* a steelhead into striking, so much so that an aroused level will cause the fish to move great distances to strike. Eggs, bobbers, and yarn do not excite steelhead to the extent that spinners do.

The above discussion has important implications for how thoroughly a particular piece of water should be fished. When I approach a particular spot, I only make enough casts to cover the spot. I then move on. This is in sharp contrast to the drift fisherman who may spend an hour fishing one run. For the latter, his bait must run very close to the fish's nose if he has any chance of getting the fish to take. This fact, coupled with a drift bait's small size, means that water will have to be worked thoroughly to be sure the run is covered. A spinner is larger, flashier, and noisier. Because it can be seen from greater distances plus the fact that it has exceptional "exciter" qualities, the angler can cover much more water with a single cast than can the drifter. The radius from which a strike can be drawn is much greater for a spinner. Experience also shows that 90 percent of the time, if a steelhead is going to strike, he will do so on the first cast into his area. Rarely will he ignore the first cast

and go for the second. This is why I only make enough casts to cover the area I am fishing. My feeling has always been that during the course of a day's fishing, my spinner may pass over many fish who ignore my offering. I don't worry about this. I expect it. I'm looking for the one, two, or three fish in my drift who are ready to strike. Having the luxury of being able to quickly cover areas with relatively few casts allows me to cover a tremendous amount of water in a short period of time. This is why a good spinner angler is always on the move, and at the same time, makes only enough casts to cover each area.

The above discussion also has important implications for the shore angler. The drift boater is not bound by physical or legal restrictions. Rivers are public property and a boat affords one the luxury of fishing just about anywhere. The shore angler is often restricted by private property, unwadeable river sections, or impenetrable shore brush. For these shore anglers, it is important to find sections of rivers which, for the most part, are easily negotiated by foot. It's pointless to drive 45 minutes to fish a 500-foot river section with spinners. You will be finished in 25 minutes. If you are a shore angler, look for large sections of river that can be waded or plan a trip for two or three smaller areas in close proximity of each other.

Exceptions and Contradictions to the "One Cast" Rule

There are exceptions and contradictions to the practice of using only enough casts to cover an area. One contradiction occurs when an angler who is fishing one spot gets a strike only after 45 minutes. This is a misleading occurrence. In his mind, the angler thinks, "It took me 45 minutes to get that darn fish to hit," and thus feels justified in making many repeated casts in the same spot. What most likely happened is that a fish moved into the drift after 45 minutes.

An exception to the one-cast rule occurs when fishing a generally turbulent area below a natural fish barrier. Fish often stack up and rest in these spots before moving upstream. The turbulence causes the fish to move instead of stay stationary. Furthermore, because there are often multiple numbers of fish, chances are good that repeated casts may eventually anger one of these fish into striking. The key here is that the turbulence causes the steelhead to change positions without spooking the fish. Any time a steelhead takes on a new resting area, he is more willing to strike. Bill Stinson in his book *Fly Rod Steelhead* addresses this phenomenon. He suggests throwing a rock near sighted fish unwilling to take in order to get them to change positions and thereby become more vulnerable to offerings. The advantage to fishing turbulent areas below fish barriers is that steelhead are forced to change positions without being spooked.

A common exception to the one-cast rule occurs when using spinners in sizes 0, 1 and 2. Because these spinners are smaller, they obviously attract from less of a radius than a larger size 3, 4 or 5. Thus, a fish may take on a second or third cast for no other reason than he did not see it the first time or was far enough away (inches?) that it did not excite the steelhead into striking. Even though much smaller, I think you will still find that even when using smaller spinners, 75 percent of your strikes will come on that first pass.

There is another consideration in this regard. That is, as you work an area, the distance between casts should be less as you go down in spinner size. In working a No. 5, I may place five feet in between casts. With a No. 2 spinner, this gets reduced to 18 inches.

Another exception to the one-cast rule occurs during weather changes. Sudden cloud coverage, sunshine, rain, increasing shadows, dawn, dusk, change of wind direction, and increased or decreased water flows can change a fish's mood. During any weather change, it is a good idea to work an area over and over during the transition in the hope of getting the fish to strike when it has been finally excited or affected by the weather change. Two memorable examples of the application of this concept come to mind.

Michigan's Ausable River has had a fine run of mostly hatchery steelhead for years. The fish are restricted to the lower six miles of the river below Foote Dam. In the lower river, water flow is regulated by the dam which is also a hydroelectric facility. Because less electricity is needed at night, the water is shut off to a trickle and the river shrinks down to practically nothing. At 8:30 a.m., the first turbine is activated and water height increases. At 10:30 a.m., the second turbine is activated and water height further increases. During each of these changes, fishing is usually very good and when each turbine is shut down later in the day, and the water level drops, the fishing action is also at a peak level.

The second example involves my initial experiences with summer steelhead in Oregon's McKenzie River. As I always keep close tabs on environmental factors, I started noticing that I consistently hooked a fish 15 minutes before the morning fog burned off. It was almost as if, when I caught a steelhead, I knew the sun was going to come out soon after. Although I have since learned to catch summer steelhead in all conditions, I still get quite a few just before the morning fog burns off the water.

It is quite common to see stationary shore anglers who have gone without a hit all day suddenly hook a fair number of fish. Weather changes can be largely responsible for this sudden increase in action. With the exception of dawn and dusk, it is impossible predict weather changes so it is pointless to be dependent upon them. Furthermore, a weather change is not always a favorable weather change. A change from a gentle westerly wind to a bitter northeasterly wind in winter is deadly. Likewise, sudden cloud cover is undesirable on water where the temperature reads 37° as is sudden sunshine when water temperature is 59°.

Sighted fish (not spawners which should be left alone) can often be negotiated on repeated casts. Steelhead are territorial about their space. Like any other wild creature, the repeated placement of something foreign which looks alive will eventually cause them to strike if not spooked first. When fishing for summer-runs, I will sometimes anchor above a tailout and to my surprise, see a steelhead lying directly below me. I'll walk a spinner down to the fish until it is an inch in front of his nose, then hold it there. This is an effective method although it is not encountered very often.

Angler Positioning

Whether fishing from shore or a boat, how you position yourself to fish an area is critical to success. Steelhead or any river fish are best enticed when the spinner swings past them at an angle. In other words, the lure is made to move mostly straight downstream and slightly laterally toward the side of the river the angler is fishing from. In most cases, this down-and-slightly-across presentation is a natural result of throwing upstream and letting the lure work through the drift. There are several reasons why this presentation is most desirable. First, a spinner that swings down but also swings laterally causes the lure's appearance, from the fish's point of view, to be constantly changing. This visual change is suggestive of life. If the fish's instinct tells him that this object floating downstream is "alive," it further induces the fish into striking. Remember how in Chapter 3 I explained that tape placed on the inside of the blade is desirable because it becomes more and less visible depending on the angle of vision? A spinner that moves down and slightly across also encourages this process. As a result, it is not only the revolving spinner blade, bright flash, or optimal color that induces a strike, but also the spinner's constantly changing visual appearance that is somewhat responsible for the steelhead's instinctive decision to strike. *This is why it is so important for the angler to position himself in a spot so that when the spinner gets close to the fish, it is moving down and slightly across.*

There are other reasons why the down-and-slightly across presentation is desirable. One reason is that during this presentation, the slight lateral movement of the spinner toward the angler may in some cases be perceived by the steelhead as the spinner's attempt to move away from the steelhead as if the steelhead is a predator. This is a further strike inducer.

Positioning yourself so that your spinner is working down and slightly across in the best portion of the drift also has other advantages that are practical in nature. First, a spinner, in this type of presentation, can be worked very deeply because water resistance will be minimized. Furthermore, a minimum of water resistance means a slower blade spin. As you will recall from an earlier discussion, a slow-spinning blade is more desirable than a fast-spinning blade.

The preferred down-and-slightly-across presentation results from the angler positioning himself *upstream* from the fish. Never stand broadside or perpendicular to the spot

A winter-run is gently guided close to shore. Asa Pearl photo

you intend to fish unless of course it is not possible to position yourself upstream. The latter type of position will greatly decrease your chances for the following reasons: 1) The spinner will never sink quickly enough to get the fish, or if it does 2) you may spook the fish via a lure splashing into the water or by having the line or lure rub against the fish's body; 3) the spinner blade will not really have had a chance to start working; 4) the spinner will almost always be moving too fast for the fish to take interest in it.

As stated above, optimal positioning is not always a possibility. Making broadside casts or retrieving from upstream is better than not fishing at all! The point is this: Never rule out a cast that can be successfully made in a likely holding area. You will soon discover that with spinners, anything is possible. I have seen steelhead chase spinners 20 feet downstream . . . right to the boat. I have also connected with five-foot casts. On one occasion, the same fish followed my spinner on two successive retrievals from upstream. But for some strange reason, the fish would not hit.

Use of common sense is very important. On small winter streams or low summer streams, get out of the boat to fish if you think that your boat's entry into the next drift may spook the fish. This is why I *always* wear waders in a boat. The ability to anchor the boat upstream and quietly approach the next pool by foot has resulted in many more takes. When I started fishing some of Oregon's tiny coastal streams, there were some spots that looked great but which never produced. Then it occurred to me that I might be spooking some of the fish with my boat so I started fishing these areas on foot! This extra bit of effort paid off!

The ability to maintain "spinner sense" is dependent upon fishing from a stationary point. Allowing the boat to slowly move in a back eddy or letting the boat move downstream as you cast will surely reduce your effectiveness and result in more snags. Effective spinner fishing for steelhead means *hard work*. On a normal-sized run, I anchor, fish, move down 20 feet, anchor, fish, etc. This is the only way to do it, folks. It can be grueling but the payoff is sweet.

Nearly every steelheader has had the experience of fishing what looks to be a great spot on one of their favorite drifts and yet is never able to hook a fish there. There are other reasons for this which will be discussed in a later chapter but one of the reasons for this phenomenon relates to boat positioning. With some spots, it does not matter where you position the boat to do your casting; with other spots, it makes

Steelhead have an awesome beauty as shown by the tail section of this summer-run. Jed Davis photo

all the difference. If you have fished what looks to be excellent holding water, drift after drift without a strike, try positioning the boat on the other side of the good water. You may get down to where the fish are more easily or the differ-

ence in presenting from the opposite side may make the spinner more attractive to fish that were always available. In some cases, a different boat position may spook the fish less than a previous position did. Only after I have tried every possible boat position five or six times will I give up on a piece of water. But it is amazing what different positioning can do for you. There have been so many cases where a different boat position turned "frog water" into prime steelhead water.

The above discussion hints of a very important concept when steelheading — *flexibility*. Because fishermen are so easily conditioned by their successes, it is often difficult to get them to explore new possibilities in lure selection, presentation, etc., when established practices have worked well. Anglers who fish for steelhead in their natural setting never really master these beautiful trout. They always are a tremendous challenge and a mystique surrounds them and the rivers they evolved from. The only chance we have for developing our potential to its fullest for catching these fish is to always be open to new ideas and possibilities. I have spinners that I designed that I know work well and, yet, I am never quite satisfied. There have been a number of instances where I developed a spinner for a certain set of conditions and said to myself, "I can't imagine a better spinner" and then two seasons later, I have to eat my words. *Comfort in the known often prevents us from discovering the unknown.* It is my feeling that a commitment to open-mindedness goes hand-in-hand with the development of steelheading technique. If you remain open to new ideas and possibilities, your steelheading may only improve five percent per year, but in ten years you will have improved 50 percent and you will probably be a true expert.

Dogs and Bears Don't Mix

I'll grant you that the above title belongs in a manual for Alaska Wilderness campers. In fact, that is where I got it from. But, I like relating this phrase to steelhead fishing. Several years ago, I did a bit of fishing with two men who had been river partners for years. One man was an expert drift fisherman — in fact, he was one of the best I have seen. His partner preferred casting lures. The drifter always outfished the lure man. After having accompanied them on several trips, the reason became quite obvious. The drifter, who always manned the oars, approached the river as a drifter would and should. He only stopped in areas that were good for pencil lead and eggs. His poor partner always got cheated as the good spinner water was always passed up. Mind you, this was not intentional. Rather, it was simply a case of the drifter not having any conception of lure fishing for steelhead.

A good spinner angler sees a river differently than does a good drift fisherman. There are countless pieces of water that a drifter would never pass up which I otherwise totally ignore. If you currently devote your time to drift fishing, a new commitment to spinner fishing will eventually reroute the way in which you approach your rivers. For this reason, it is important that in fishing spinners, you should drift with partners who also see rivers in terms of spinners. A die-hard drifter simply does not know how to approach potential spinner water. In fact, if I am invited to fish with someone who I know is a confirmed drifter, I don't bring along any spinners. I get out the old pencil lead and Glo-Gos.

Chapter 6

Steelhead, Environment, and Basic Spinner Strategy

WHILE BOTH THIS AND THE PRECEDING chapter discuss the basics of river fishing for steelhead, the types of issues addressed in both chapters are vastly different. The preceding chapter dealt primarily with how to swim a spinner through a river. This chapter focuses on the steelhead's ever-changing river environment and how this influences spinner selection. However, content is not the only difference between the two chapters. In Chapter 2, we dealt with steelheading constants — that is, aspects of technique that never really change. An example is our "down-and-slightly-across" presentation and the angler's striving to fish the spinner near the bottom. While the mastery of these techniques is paramount, their practice becomes second nature with experience. This chapter looks at ever-changing environmental variables and how we select spinners to accommodate any one set of variables. Herein lies the *ultimate* challenge of steelhead spinner fishing: a constant battle of wits with an unpredictable Mother Nature and her hard-to-get prize: Steelhead.

Upon starting a day of fishing, many steelheaders open their tackle boxes and, while staring into them, try to figure out what the fish are biting. Lure selection is a never-ending search for the "magic lure" that will "catch fish." Such random lure selection is based on little more than superstition and personal mood. Anglers who fish this way really believe that steelheading success is a question of luck. From my point of view, luck plays a small part in steelheading success. When steelhead are in our streams in fishable numbers, only fish size is consistently based on luck. Consistent success is maybe 10 percent luck and the more I fine-tune my own technique, the more I rediscover this fact.

There are five environmental factors that will, to a large degree, determine spinner size and degree of brightness/gaudiness. These are water temperature, water clarity, prevailing light conditions, water height, and river size. These factors will guide you in selection, thereby eliminating the guesswork from steelhead spinner fishing. To measure these factors, only one nonhuman tool is needed: a simple water thermometer. Through reading the following chapters on winter and summer steelhead, plus individual experience on your own streams, you will learn which spinners correspond to various combinations of the above factors. Instead of changing lures every 30 minutes to see "what the fish are biting," a single measure of water temperature, a look into the sky, and a glance into the water will tell you what to use. And, as conditions may change throughout the day, your awareness of changing daylight or increased water temperature will allow you to keep on adjusting spinner selection to match conditions. The result is that except for challenging borderline cases or unusual circumstances, you can be fishing one-hundred percent effectively from your first cast on. This means more action and few skunked days!

Our goal, then, is to eliminate guessing games and purposeless lure selection and replace it with a systematic, foolproof system that is reliable (but not magical). In this way, we take the luck out of steelheading.

Let's first explore each of the five environmental factors and then see how the sum of these factors dictates the use of a particular spinner.

Steelhead and Water Temperature

The most important and reliable predictor of spinner size and finish is water temperature. A day of steelhead fishing should always begin with a temperature reading. This will immediately put you in touch with the steelhead's underwater environment and thereby give you *the most important* clue as to the range of spinners to be used. As the day progresses, temperature readings should be taken at approximately two-hour intervals. A rising hot sun or a sudden cold wind can certainly influence water temperature. Daytime water temperatures generally fluctuate two to four or even six degrees. In desert steelhead streams like the Deschutes, water temperature fluctuations can be much greater. In certain temperature ranges, a two-degree shift is very significant but in other temperature ranges a six-degree shift may have little or no significance with regard to a change in spinners.

The temperature range from which most steelhead strains can be successfully angled is 33° to 62°F. Below 33° produces ice. At 62° and beyond, most West-of-the-Cascades or "coastal" strains of steelhead start to experience discomfort and their propensity to hit (unless forced to via unethical practices) begins to diminish. More importantly, a steelhead that has expended considerable energy in such warm water has a decreasing chance of surviving if released. The State of Indiana's summer steelhead are a good example of this. The water temperature in the small streams the fish use to migrate to the hatcheries from which they were released is usually 62° to 65°. Indiana Department of Natural Resources personnel advise anglers *not* to release fish because they have no chance of making it once they have expended considerable energy in such warm water.

The most important temperature ranges and cutoffs are 33° to 42°, 43° to 49°, 50° to 53°, 54° to 57°, and 58° to 60°. Within each temperature range, we are *always* striving to reach the threshold of attraction by selecting the largest and gaudiest spinners that will attract almost to the point of spooking the steelhead. By using the maximum size, we can attract from a greater periphery.

In the 33° to 42° range, steelhead metabolism will be low.

The use of a simple water thermometer is critical for summer steelhead success when using spinners. Jed Davis photo

The fish will generally be lethargic, slower, less eager to strike, and less prone to chase spinners over long distances. In this range, steelhead are also not spooked as easily due to their lowered metabolism. Thus, we have to compensate for a low-metabolized state by presenting a spinner that produces maximum flash and gaudiness such that fish will be excited into chasing and striking. Silver-plated No. 5s are used just about exclusively unless fish have been harassed by anglers or the stream is ridiculously low, clear, or small. In this lower temperature range, it will be a rare circumstance in which you question the use of the larger size 4 or 5s.

In the 43° to 49° range, which is considered a normal winter range, No. 5s are generally preferred by experts although silver-plated No. 4s will be needed where circumstances are causing fish to spook more easily. Again, this may be due to harassment, low/clear water, or stream size. I would say that No. 4s are the most commonly store-bought size in the Northwest. In terms of flash and gaudiness, they can excite steelhead almost as much as No. 5s do. I prefer No. 5s because the added weight allows me to fish more effectively in the deeper holes. In the smaller streams, No. 4s can match the performance of No. 5s but, on the normal-sized or larger streams, I would go with No. 5s for the most effective fishing.

From 50° on, spinner selection changes considerably and becomes much more complicated. Steelhead metabolism increases considerably relative to the lower temperature ranges. The fish are more easily spooked and thus more influenced by other environmental factors. Extra care must be taken to select spinners that do not go beyond the threshold of attraction.

The 50° to 53° range is a transitional range that is highly variable. Selecting the optimal spinner for any given set of conditions within this temperature range can be difficult, tricky, and a tremendous challenge. I've taken fish with spinners ranging from a black No. 2 to a silver-plated No. 5. Individual circumstances will be discussed in detail in the next two chapters.

In the 54° to 57° range, steelhead become hair-trigger torpedoes. They are super sensitive to any environmental influence and are very easily spooked. It takes very little to excite them into striking and extreme caution must be taken not to go beyond the threshold of attraction. This means that No. 2s will be used much of the time with some use of No. 3s and 4s. Silver is out in most cases. Purposely-tarnished brass, shiny brass, copper, and black oxide are in.

The 58° to 62° range is much like the preceding temperature range. Steelhead are very sensitive but even more so. This is where you will start wanting to use a lot No. 0s and 1s.

Beyond 62°, I either look for a cooler river or concentrate my efforts on other species. In temperatures of 62° on, the coastal steelhead's willingness to strike drops off considerably, probably because the fish is most concerned with survival due to the discomfort that warm water temperatures produce. They will hit occasionally but will most likely be somewhat lethargic. However, it must be noted that strains of steelhead from east of the Cascades have a slightly greater tolerance and will readily strike in temperatures of 70°.

It must be stressed that the temperature guidelines outlined above are general guidelines designed to provide orientation and give you a framework to work with. You may be confronted with an unusual set of circumstances that, for example, may require the use of a larger spinner in 55° - 60° water. So remain flexible in your experimentation. Exceptions are the rule in any type of steelheading.

Water Clarity

This is one environmental variable that most steelheaders are pretty well tuned into. A general rule exists: The greater the water visibility, the smaller and less gaudy the spinner. For example, when a river is lowering and just coming into shape, the largest fluorescent Glo-Go might be used by the drifter. As the water clears, bobber size drops accordingly. With spinners, the same pattern follows. For example, in otherwise clear winter rivers where No. 4 spinners are used, a No. 5 would be used if the water becomes off-colored. If I am already using a No. 5 in a clear winter stream (perhaps due to a very cold water temperature), then off-colored conditions will obviously not change the size spinner I use. However, I might employ a brighter fluorescent tape.

Water clarity plays a large role in spinner selection for summer steelhead rivers that run off-colored. Two examples are Oregon's South Santiam and Deschutes rivers. During the summer, I fish both the South Santiam and McKenzie rivers for Skamania strain steelhead. The McKenzie runs gin-clear all summer but the Santiam is always a bit off-colored due to the Monmerlite clay deposit in the South Santiam's source, Green Peter Reservoir. Instead of settling, this clay remains in suspension, the result being that the South Santiam always has a greenish, off-colored cast. Because the water is an off-colored green, less direct sunlight penetrates the water and fish therefore have a greater sense of security and are less spooky. The threshold of attraction is higher and I therefore will use large, gaudier spinners. For comparison, I often use a No. 2 black-bladed spinner in the McKenzie when angling in 54° water in direct sunlight. Under the same conditions on the Santiam, I go with a No. 3 brass with fluorescent kelly-green adornments. The No. 3 brass would spook McKenzie steelhead under these gin-clear conditions but because of lessened water clarity in the Santiam, a larger spinner does the best job. This is not to say that a No. 2 black will not work under these Santiam conditions. It will. However, it will be less effective since it will not attract from as great a periphery.

Prevailing Light Conditions

Available lighting plays a large role in spinner selection as the water climbs above 50°. In fact, with each higher degree of water temperature above 50°, steelhead become increasingly more sensitive to lighting conditions. Therefore, spinner selection must correspond to these temperature changes when angling in various light conditions.

Winter steelhead are generally taken in waters less than 50°. While holding in the most common 43° to 49° range, bright sunlight may cause fish to be a touch more cautious. However, in the long run, the presence or absence of clouds should not make a significant difference in the spinners you are using unless you are fishing a very small, shallow, or clear stream where fish are highly visible or unless you are angling in a stream where there has been constant heavy boat traffic. Many winter steelheaders see direct sunlight as a sign of bad steelheading and therefore develop a psychological block to fishing under cloudless skies. As a result, they have less confidence and start fishing half-heartedly and therefore less effectively. Unless you are on a stream with extremely intense angling pressure or boat traffic, direct sunlight should never be a significant obstacle when fishing any steelhead waters under 50°. Most importantly, it should not influence spinner selection. For example, if I am fishing a normal-sized stream with normal boat traffic, the sudden clouds will not cause me to switch to a No. 5 from a No. 4. When angling in waters below 43°, sunlight actually helps! A bright wintry sun will warm the water, thus helping to increase steelhead metabolism, the result being that the fish will become more active and willing to strike.

From 50° to 53°, sunlight has a significant effect and this effect is greater for temperatures of 52° and 53° than it is for 50° and 51° temperatures. Once again, this transitional stage can make spinner selection complicated. Depending upon other factors, lighting conditions within this range may have a significant effect. At other times, they have little effect. Specific circumstances will be dealt with in the following chapters.

From 54° to 62°, constant awareness of prevailing lighting conditions will pay large dividends to the angler. During thick cloud cover, at dawn, or at dusk, No. 3s and even some No. 4s can be used. But as soon as that sun hits the water, larger spinners become useless pieces of hardware on the typical clear summer stream. Angling in 54° and up with direct sunlight, the general rule is small, dark, and dull. This is where the use of No. 1 and 2 size spinners can produce some dynamite steelheading. Black blades and purposely-tarnished brass and copper play a large role in my steelheading when angling under these conditions. Sunlight and high-range temperatures are dealt with in great detail in the summer steelhead chapter.

Water Height

Water height is another environmental factor that most steelheaders are attuned to. However, the exclusive use of fluctuating water height, except in extreme circumstances, is a poor indicator of which size spinner should be used for *winter steelhead*. This belief comes from experience. Here in the Northwest, as in the Great Lakes, there are periods of time, during the winter when no rain falls for a two- or three-week period. Rivers recede to a low level. You would think that spinner size would have to go down but, in most circumstances, this is not the case. Why? That can be answered in two words: water temperatures. Even if a winter river recedes to a low winter level, water temperature is not likely to increase because cool winter air will keep the temperature down. Cold winter waters in the 30s and 40s will slow down steelhead metabolism and the fish will be less spooky. As long as the fish have a sense of security and have not been harassed, large gaudy spinners will be most effective in exciting the steelhead. Here in Oregon, I fish a number of tiny coastal streams. I never fail to be amazed at the fact that I can use No. 5s with excellent results. However, if the water temperatures of these streams started to climb into the 50s, it would be a different story altogether.

For summer steelhead, water height is a bit more meaningful of an indicator of spinner size although it, too, is only a marginal indicator. Rivers, in summer, recede to extremely low levels relative to their winter levels. This means that fish are extremely vulnerable. As a result, they are super wary and easily spooked by too large an offering. However, much of their wariness and being highly spook-prone is due to high water temperatures which often go hand-in-hand with low water. Again, *it is water temperature, not the low water*, that is the primary consideration for spinner selection; but, because most anglers do not take water temperature readings, they associate their success on small spinners or "low water" flies with low water height which is always visible when fishing — hence the illusion. In situations where a cold front cools off the water that otherwise remains low, larger spinners will become quite effective.

Water height is also confused with water clarity. In winter, high water usually means less clarity and lower water generally means clearer waters. It is the clarity, not the height, that influences spinner selection or bait selection of any type. This is because steelhead seek the same depth and flow (assuming it is available) within a given temperature range regardless of river height. Whether the river is one foot higher or two feet lower makes no difference. If waters recede, this doesn't mean the fish holds in shallow water. Instead, he seeks a deeper hole in which he can attain the same depth, current, and *degree of safety. Thus, you angle for the fish under similar conditions even though the river is lower.* Hence, there is no reason to switch spinner sizes. However, if the same water has less clarity, a larger offering may be desirable for greater visibility over a wider range.

River Size

A lot of steelheaders will consider river size when trying to gauge what kind of fly or lure to use. The reasoning here is that fish that have more room will be less spooky and thus will more actively pursue an offering. In my opinion, river size is a highly overrated factor in most circumstances. This belief comes from experience. I have spinner fished winter steelhead rivers in Oregon and Michigan that were 20 feet across or only large enough to accommodate an 8-foot pram, and yet have done quite well with No. 4s and 5s.

Two points are to be made here. First, river size, in and of itself, only seems to be a factor if the river is exceptionally tiny, exceptionally low (drought), or angling pressure causes the fish to be constantly spooked or wary of angler presence. Michigan's Upper Platte River is an excellent example of this phenomenon. On April 1st of every year, this small but beautiful stream opens up to anglers. From 5:00 a.m. on, it's like a German blitzkrieg. Hordes of anglers from Michigan, New York, Ohio, and Pennsylvania converge on the stream. The water is generally clear and the fish cannot escape angler presence. There is simply nowhere to go. Constant harassment, in concert with unethical and illegal fishing practices, makes the fish extremely wary. In the early 1970s, a time before steelhead were discovered in Michigan, it was quite easy to tease steelhead out of the larger holes with No. 4 and 5 spinners. Under present conditions, I don't think I would fish anything other than a No. 2 or 3. However, there are a number of tiny, lesser

known streams such as the Crockery, North Branch Pentwater, and North Branch White that can be fished quite productively with larger spinners.

The second point is that river size is often confused with river clarity. The Deschutes River is a larger river but the reason steelhead can be taken with large Stee-lees, Tadpollys, and spinners in the middle of a hot summer day is due to water clarity, not river size. The Deschutes runs off-colored with 5-foot visibility. If the lower river ran clear, angling practices on the Deschutes would be quite different. Spinner selection is much more influenced by water clarity than it is by river size and height.

Other Factors to Consider

Two additional factors deserve mention: air temperature and wind direction. In most cases, these two factors have marginal significance but, in special circumstances, they can help to explain a shift in steelhead behavior or negotiability.

Air temperature is the Fool's Gold of steelheading. The reason for this is simple. *Steelhead live in water, not air.* Does air temperature have an effect? Yes, but indirectly. Air temperature is significant to the extent that it warms or cools the water, but a particular air temperature does not always correspond to the same water temperature. Two examples demonstrate this. On the summer streams I fish, a dawn air temperature reading of 38° usually means that the water temperature will be somewhere around 49° to 51°. A January dawn air temperature reading of 38° often means that the temperature of my winter streams will be somewhere between 42° and 48°. Thus, if I were to use air temperature as a gauge of where the fish are and what spinner to use, I would be fishing ineffectively in at least one of these two circumstances. This is a classic example of why air temperature is a misleading, if not useless, consideration on a day-to-day basis.

However, there is one circumstance under which air temperature will tell you something. This occurs when the air is colder than the water. This is generally the result of unseasonal air temperatures or early morning temperatures. It changes the typical almost-constant air temperature/water temperature relationship (i.e., water colder than the air) that fish seem to feel more comfortable in. Fish often respond to this air/water relationship change by laying low and going off the bite. This does not mean that fishing is a waste of time. It does mean that the potential for a truly good day is reduced. Jock Scott, in his book *Greased Line Fishing for Salmon*, alludes to this phenomenon although more in reference to the Atlantic salmon's unresponsiveness to flies presented at or below the surface when air is colder than water. Why fish react poorly to the warmer-water/colder-air phenomenon is not known. We do know, however, that they must feel uncomfortable in some way because their willingness to strike is reduced.

I am particularly sensitive to this phenomenon when going after summer-runs in September and October. The typical summer river temperature for the McKenzie is 54°. If one night the air temperature suddenly drops to 35°, this means that, if I start fishing at dawn, the air will be colder than the water for a number of hours. With such a set of circumstances, I will plan my drift for later in the day or I won't go at all.

This same phenomenon is common to winter steelheading. Typically, super-cold nights will cause the air to be colder than the water for the initial hours of a steelhead day. Thus, it comes as no surprise that steelheading often improves as the day progresses. Bill Luch, in *Steelhead Drift Fishing*, says a few words on this, although, interestingly, I don't know if he is aware that this phenomenon relates to the air/water relationship:

Time after time the [winter steelhead] fishing, under otherwise perfect conditions, hasn't become really good until the sun hit the water – or at least until full light of day. Many times, I have hit the stream at the crack of dawn, only to have my first fish around 8:30 or 9:00 in the morning.

Wind direction can also have an influence. Easterly winds rarely produce good fishing of any kind. I may think twice about a day of steelhead fishing if strong easterly winds are predicted in the weather forecast. Westerly, northerly, and southerly winds are most desirable. Westerly are the best. A shift from west to east, during the course of a day's fishing, is often deadly. A shift from east to west usually turns the fish on. When the water is cold and steelhead metabolism low, a sudden warm wind can often help to put them on the bite. A cold wind, regardless of direction, has a similar effect on summer-runs if preceding temperatures were in the 90s or low 100s. This is an interesting phenomenon because it takes a good amount of time for a sudden air temperature change to actually cool or warm the water. The sudden shift probably has a favorable barometric effect that gets the fish moving.

The overall point is that air temperature and wind direction should not be used to determine spinner selection. They are factors that, in most cases, have only a minor influence on steelhead fishing. However, a casual awareness of their presence and change may not only help explain why fish are not biting or stopped biting, but also help you pick the best days to try your luck.

Putting It All Together

Effective steelhead spinner fishing starts with consideration of the environment. On each and every day I fish a river, the first thing I do is take a water temperature reading. I then check out water clarity and available lighting. During the course of the entire day, I will be taking water temperature readings at two-hour intervals and/or after every hooked fish. Although my concentration will be focused on actual fishing, not one moment will pass where I am not aware of a change in lighting – be it shadows, or the emergence of clouds or sun. The result of paying close attention to these factors will not only result in an ever-increasing understanding of steelhead behavior but it will also result in knowing exactly which size, finish, and color spinner is best suited for a particular set of circumstances. The result of doing this will lead you to growing confidence, consistent action, few skunked days, and a tremendous feeling of satisfaction.

Each time you hook a fish, take a water temperature reading, record the available lighting, and take note of the water clarity. In addition, make a mental note of the exact *type* of water you hooked your fish in. This should include an estimation of the depth of the water, the speed, and the character of the water surface; that is, was the surface

smooth, slightly broken, heavily chopped, or riffled? Be sure to include any outstanding characteristics of the spot where you hooked your fish — i.e., behind a rock, next to a sunken log, over small stones. Finally, record the spinner you used to hook your fish. Take a small notebook to the stream or jot down everything as soon as you get home.

The author tails a steelhead on Oregon's Yachats. Asa Pearl photo

With your first few fish, each individual recording will seem meaningless and you may wonder if recording all this data has any point. But as you accumulate more data, patterns will start to emerge that will eventually guide you in spinner selection and, hence, fishing 100 percent effectively all the time. The first thing that you are likely to discover is that, when using a favored spinner, most of your fish will come from a consistent set of circumstances. Thus, when you encounter an unusual circumstance or fish, you will begin to experiment until you've found the right spinner. When that same circumstance arises at a later time, you will know exactly what to do. This is the beauty of recording the conditions in which you take each steelhead because with a couple of years of experimentation, you will have encountered and solved situations and, if you do get skunked (everyone does at least once or twice a year . . . repeat, everyone), at least you will have the satisfaction of knowing that you were fishing effectively with proven methods.

Understanding fully well that most anglers do not "fish

with the environment," I would like to end this chapter with four real-life stream situations so that you can see how I use the environment to select spinners. There is really nothing very difficult about selecting spinners this way. However, to develop a feel for this approach does take time, experience, and patience for which there is absolutely no substitute!

Case 1

Winter steelhead; medium-sized stream, shallow. No rain for 18 days, water super low by winter standards, and gin-clear. Sunny, water temperature 48°. Normally use a No. 5 silver but because of extreme conditions, I go to a No. 4 silver or a No. 3 silver.

Case 1A

Return to river the following day. Still no rain, but total cloud cover and water temperature drops to 44° due to very cold night. I go with No. 5 silver because fish not as spooky due to clouds and lowered metabolism via 4° drop in temperature.

Case 2

Summer steelhead; medium-sized stream at normal summer height. Water clear and at 54°. Low cloud and fog cover. Perfect for No. 3 brass. Steelhead spooked by larger spinner and can get sufficient depth with No. 3. Silver too flashy.

Case 2A

Sun burns off clouds by 10:00 a.m., now total sunshine. Temperature up to 57°. Fish ultra-spooky in these circumstances. Must use small spinner with dull finish. Go to No. 2 with black blade and tarnished brass body.

Case 2B

Later in day, arrive at fast, deep run where steelhead hold before moving upstream. Temperature still at 57°, total sunshine but run is totally shaded. Go to No. 3 brass because fish less spooky here plus I need greater depth and visibility. After I'm out of shade, switch back to No. 2 black-bladed spinner.

Case 3

Winter steelhead: Fishing tiny coastal tributary, only 15 feet wide. Water temperature at 46°. Sunny. Stream beginning to clear but still off-colored. Even though stream is a twinkie, fish feel secure due to cover of off-colored water. Go with a No. 3 silver.

Case 3A

Same as above but clouds over later in day. Switch to No. 4.

Case 3B

Same as 3A except stream receiving heavy pressure. Go to a No. 2 silver. If stream clears even more, go to a No. 2 brass.

Case 3C

Return to same stream one week later. Temperature 48°. Cloudy. Water is gin-clear. Fish visible, aware of my presence. Go with No. 2 brass. Two hours go by no luck. Go to No. 2 tarnished brass. Still no luck after two hours and many sighted fish. Switch to No. 2 with black blade. Finally get strikes. Fish obviously getting lots of pressure. Ultra-spooky due to vulnerability.

Case 4

Summer steelhead: Large, off-colored river. Visibility six feet. 54°. Sunny. Select No. 4 brass. Fish well-covered by off-colored water. Visibility lower so large spinner will not spook and is needed for peripheral attraction.

Case 4A

Same as above but at dusk. Go to a No. 5 silver plate. Darker lighting, fish even less spooky so the No. 5 works very well.

This large summer steelhead was taken on a No. 1 McKenzie Dark. The fish bit on a clear sunny tailout in the middle of the day, clear evidence that being on the water at 4:00 a.m. is not a necessity for taming wary summer-runs. Jed Davis photo

Chapter 7

Winter Steelhead

DURING MY LAST DAY OF FISHING IN Michigan, I came across a man who, like myself, was trying to squeeze every bit out of what was now a waning spring steelhead season. But for me, there was really more at stake. I would be moving far away from Michigan in just a few weeks. And, while I was excited about the prospect of living in — and especially of steelhead fishing in — the Pacific Northwest, it was now the end of an era in my life. A state called Michigan and its fish, the steelhead trout, had given me a direction and purpose in life. I kept reminiscing that day from a treasure chest of experiences that spanned three decades and many hours of devotion. I started to speak with the other angler. We asked each other a few questions. He then commented: "We're pretty well into spring and I could go for other fish, but these steelhead, they just seem to get into your blood, don't they?"

I never forgot this man and I never forgot his words because they touched a soft spot deep inside. They seemed to get me in touch with what winter steelhead mean to me. It is difficult for me to describe just what those feelings are. But, like many steelheaders, I do know that I always have to keep fishing for them.

There is much more to winter steelhead fishing than most people think. Generations of drift fishermen and plug-pullers have narrowed our concept of where winter steelhead hold, what they will hit, and how aggressive they really are. Part of this results from the limitations of drift gear itself which dictates a minimal current as well as a relatively snag-free bottom. The result is that fishing is confined to classic drift water.

Spinner fishing for steelhead has a different feel altogether. Snaggy bottoms and minimal currents do not impede the ability to effectively fish. What to the drift fisherman is a no-no becomes a distinct possibility to the spinner fisherman. For the spinner angler, *rivers are seen differently* and

the concept of "the best steelhead water" does not necessarily coincide with the drifter's dream drift. But, as I pointed out in an earlier chapter, each method has its advantages and disadvantages. Spinners are no exception. We spinner anglers have our problems, too, and this must be taken into account as we plan strategy.

In this chapter, we take a close look at winter steelhead. We'll look at their behavior and how this behavior changes with changing river conditions. And, we'll take a look at terminal tackle in terms of what spinners are well-matched to various conditions. I suppose that there may be a strong urge to discover "what the secret lure is" and make light of all this steelhead behavior talk. As I have repeatedly said throughout this book, effective steelhead fishing starts with a good understanding of the fish — not with the best lures. This means knowing how the steelhead responds to changes in his environment. Only then can one make intelligent choices about lure selection. And only then does one know where to put that lure. To arbitrarily choose what you think is the magical spinner and then fish it without having a feel for the fish and their behavior is pointless and will lead to erratic results. Trying to fish steelhead without having an understanding of their behavior is like trying to read a book without knowing what the words mean. You will go crazy if you randomly select "good-looking" spinners in the hope that one will be the end-all answer. You have to start with steelhead behavior. So let's begin . . .

The Upstream Journey

When a steelhead, fresh from the ocean, enters a river, it has two concerns on its upstream journey — *rest* and *safety*. Although predators were everywhere, the ocean-going steelhead had an almost limitless area within which to seek safety. The steelhead now enters a river with every limited depth and width — hence, the wariness, caution, and a pre-occupation with *safety*. As the steelhead works its way up-stream, powerful gushes of water from swollen winter streams tax stored energy and stamina. If the steelhead is to make it past each of the upstream obstacles that separate him from his spawning ground, he will need to recharge with *rest* at various points in his journey.

Three factors, in general, determine when the steelhead migrates upstream. These are water temperature, water height, and water clarity. When water temperature drops below 40°, all activity ceases. Steelhead will not move regardless of circumstance. From 42° on up, the steelhead move as other conditions permit. These conditions are first, water height and second, water clarity. Available lighting is also a factor. A minimally increased water level, of course, is desirable for fish to move. (In extreme circumstances of drought, steelhead will move when they have to.) However, I have found that this minimal level can be somewhat compensated for by the water's off-colored cast. This fact was driven home to me several years ago on Oregon's Yachats River. A two-week drying trend had put the rivers at a low and clear level. We were finally blessed with a half-inch of rain one evening. I arrived at the Yachats the next morning. The water had risen four or five inches so I did not have great expectations for the coming day. I hooked one dark steelhead early in the drift. When I approached the lower part of the drift, I started to get into very fresh steelhead. I ended up hooking five and landing four on spinners. A great day but why had the steelhead moved with such a slight increase in water height? Two reasons came to mind: First, run-off had transferred the river from gin-clear to off-colored; hence, the steelhead had a greater sense of security. Second, it was a dark day with a constant "peach-fuzz" drizzle. I have to believe that low-light conditions augmented the fish's decision to move freely.

It is when steelhead are migrating that they become most vulnerable to our offerings. Any time a steelhead has recently moved into a new holding position, this is when he will be most aggressive, less picky, and more negotiable for a greater period of time during the day. It is when a steelhead has held for one or two weeks in the same position that it becomes "stale" and, at times, almost impossible to catch. These stale times usually occur during low, gin-clear water conditions. I've drifted Oregon rivers at extremely low levels where I spotted thirty or forty steelhead and, yet, couldn't get them to take interest in anything.

Each stream has a certain level where anglers have deemed the river as "in" or as "fishable." This usually corresponds to a river level in which a large number of fish are moving but where the water is low enough so that fish are congregated in fishable numbers and where the water is clear enough so that steelhead have enough visibility to spot our offerings from a reasonable distance. While this is an optimal time to be on the river, don't confine your angling to these conditions only. Some of my greatest catches have come from far less than optimal conditions.

For example, it is known that a warm winter rain will warm up estuaries to above 40° such that large numbers of steelhead will be triggered to move. As the river level drops, an abundance will be distributed in the river. However, let's say that during a two-week drying and warming trend, the estuary warms to 42° and the river is even warmer. Further-more, it just so happens that a number of steelhead are ready to move into the river. Then it is possible for there to be good numbers of fresh steelhead even though there was no rainfall at all. Thus, while rainfall is a good indicator of steelhead movement and fishing prospects, it doesn't tell the whole story.

Two Key Environmental Factors

Two environmental factors play a large role in determining where winter steelhead hold. These are water temperature and water height. However, don't be confused. In the previous chapter, I didn't give much importance to water height but that was for *spinner selection*. For determining where steelhead hold, it is a very important consideration. Let's explore the factors and then see how they work together.

As noted in an earlier chapter, the typical winter steelhead water temperature range is 33° to 49°. While spinner selection does not significantly vary within this range, the behavior of winter steelhead does. I like to divide this temperature range into three categories: 33° to 39°, 40° to 43°, and 44° to 49°.

From 33° to 39°, steelhead tend to be lethargic and their metabolism is at its lowest point. A steelhead, regardless of any environmental factors, always holds in moving water. But in this low temperature range, they are often found in the slower-moving water of a particular run. The tendency of many anglers is to work the center of a run really hard in the belief that the steelhead will always be there. Not so. When the thermometer dips, they can be found in the following types of places: on the edge of fast water and slower-moving water; on the periphery of a run where the water flows at a half or two-thirds the speed of the faster water; among submerged boulders at least three feet deep in slow-moving water without any break on the water's surface; under a log or undercut bank, both of which are in places where slow-moving water passes; toward and in the tail of a pool where water slows. The types of water in which steelhead are less likely to hold in are: the head of a pool; fast, shallow riffles; any water with a heavy-riffled surface; fast water in general. Mind you, this is not to say that I won't fish the head of a pool or the riffles. What it does mean is that I will spend less time in these places and budget more time to the slower water.

From 40° to 43°, winter steelhead can be in any type of moving water although they will have a slight tendency to seek out the more slow to moderate currents. Like the 50° to 53° range for selecting spinners, this lower range can make steelheading difficult in the sense that with a limited number of available fish, it will be more difficult to find fish that can be in slower or faster water. In such a circumstance, I like to select a short drift and work it thoroughly.

From 44° to 49° and even to 50°, steelhead are usually to be found in and around the areas of greatest flow — unless of course these areas have too strong a current. In this temperature range, steelhead will stay within the mainstream of a particular run. While steelhead occasionally hold in slower water, I generally stick to the faster water. But remember, it is quite common to have a steelhead follow a spinner from faster to slower water and then strike in the slower water. This is why it is so important to let your spinner work directly downstream and then wind in slowly for ten feet before giving up on the cast.

In the common 44° to 49° range, steelhead have preference for water with a broken surface. Shallow water of three feet or less is referred to as "riffles." Broken water deeper than three feet is called "chop." Quite commonly then we will see steelhead holding toward the head or center of a pool where there is the greatest amount of chop provided that the water is not too fast. Thus, it comes as no surprise that between 44° and 49°, steelhead like to hold in the mainstream of the run.

Water height also has a significant effect on where steelhead like to hold. When water is high, cocoa brown, with little visibility, steelhead are experiencing some discomfort. Dirt mixed with water gets into their gill rakers and probably has somewhat of a suffocating effect. In this instance, the steelhead's main concern is to seek cleaner, clearer water which may be found close to shore and out of the main current or in smaller tributaries. While most anglers don't bother fishing in these conditions, most of the fish, if any are to be caught, can be found close into shore — sometimes right on the river's edge. This is why plunkers can have good luck in high water. In these high, off-colored conditions, I personally head for a smaller tributary — either one that clears more quickly or one so tiny that even when off-colored, it is fishable.

As the river levels drop and the water is on the verge of turning from brown to green or as in the case of the Great Lakes, red-brown to translucent roily brown, the fish begin to move more easily. I like to think of a steelhead river as a series of pools, each one a step of a staircase that eventually leads to the fish's destination, his spawning ground. The great majority of steelhead are taken within the framework of a pool. And, thus, it is important to understand what a pool is and how it relates to water height.

A pool is created by a sudden drop in elevation of the stream bed. Gravity increases the speed of water and a ridge of gushing white water is formed. At the point where the white water apron disappears is the point where the pool begins. This point and the section of the pool extending usually one-third of the way down the pool is referred to as the "head." The head is characterized as the fastest-flowing water of the pool. The middle third of the pool is called the "drift." This section is similar to the head although it is deeper, less turbulent, and the water slows down. From the point where the water starts to shallow out until the next drop in elevation is referred to as the "tail" or "tailout." This water is generally very smooth, and becomes progressively shallower. Also, water tends to gain speed as it passes through the tail. The point at which tailout water turns into white water is referred to as the "break." At the break, a drop in elevation once again forms white water which starts another pool. Just as Manx cats have no tails, some "species" of pools have no tails either. Instead, the drift opens up into a lake-like body of water that has no definition and little speed. This is referred to as "frog water." It is good for "boondoggling," i.e., trolling eggs or spinners off the bottom as you move along; in general, it does not offer consistent results

As water clears sufficiently, steelhead begin ascending the pools. In the initial clearing stages, the water is still a bit high (although fishable) and most likely has an off-colored cast. This is a time when steelhead are most commonly holding in the tail of the pool. Having just negotiated the white water of the previous pool, the steelhead

immediately seeks rest before moving on. Steelhead, because of their body shape, find it very easy to hold in the fast, slick water of a tailout and, because the water's height and muddled clarity provide a shield of safety, the fish feel quite comfortable here.

As the water drops and clears to what would be considered a normal winter level, steelhead move into the drift. For obvious reasons, clearing water and a drop in water level deem steelhead very vulnerable in the tail. The drift is faster, deeper, and with enough surface turbulence to provide a shield of safety. Of course, this is not to say that steelhead will not be in the tail when the water clears and lowers. They will, but to a lesser degree. In addition, any fish holding in the tail will become more cautious and less likely to hit. This is why I don't concentrate too much fishing effort on tailout sections in normal to low water conditions. For these conditions, I think they are a bit overrated.

The Alsea River is among the best producers in North America. The author shows off a fine fish taken from a popular spot. David Davis photo

While winter is the season for precipitation, we do have two- and three-week drying trends. At such times, streams will recede to low winter levels. Tailouts may become mere trickles that would never hold a fish and "drift" sections are often too slow and shallow for steelhead. It is during times like these that steelhead often move into the heads of pools. They seek out the faster water with riffles and chop *that is equal in speed, flow, and protection to other parts of the pool at a higher river height.* Such water need not be deep. However, it does need to have speed and a broken surface to give the steelhead a sense of security. Anyone who has been a reader of *Salmon Trout Steelheader* magazine is well-acquainted with occasional references or articles on the frustrations of angling for winter steelhead in low water. Supposedly, "fish will not bite in low water or are unavailable, if not depleted." This has not been my experience. My observation is that anglers fish for low-water winter-runs in the wrong places. Through convention and conditioning, the river is fished exactly the same way without regard to river stage. The common-sense logic is that steelhead will seek out the same areas over and over again. This is true *if* the water levels stay the same. In low river levels, the relationship of steelhead to its river changes and the angler must make the accommodation. In low water, tailouts and lower sections of the "drift" offer little in the way of action on most normal-sized streams and, yet, you see all sorts of anglers working this water seriously, just waiting for and expecting a strike.

If we take a look at water temperature in tandem with water height, steelhead behavior is more easily understood. This helps us to pinpoint, on any given day, where the greater numbers of steelhead may be holding and, thus, allows us to concentrate our efforts accordingly. Perhaps the best way of describing the relationship of these two factors is by discussing some typical examples using a normal-sized winter steelhead river.

Unhooking a very late winter-run. The author fishes Oregon winter-runs through April, a time when most anglers are long gone. Asa Pearl photo

In the 33° to 39° range, high water is likely to put steelhead in very slow-moving, almost-slack water. This water can often be found close to shore or to the side of a main run. Tailout fish would be common although the fish would not be holding in the faster portion of the tail. They would be off to the side where slower water is better matched to their metabolism. As the water lowered to normal levels, I would still expect to find steelhead in the peripheral areas although not to the same extent. Very slow-moving, almost-slack water would make the steelhead too vulnerable but, just the same, concentrating heavily on the fast portion of the drift is not likely to produce fantastic results either. In very low water, the fish may move into deeper or faster water for safety reasons. However, they probably will not be in the riffles or turbulent chop. The water is simply too much for their lowered metabolism. This presents a problem in very tiny streams, those that are usually walked. A steelhead's willingness to hit is dependent upon the fish feeling safe. In tiny, low-water streams with temperatures in the mid-thirties, a lowered metabolism forces the fish to lie in more vulnerable places that provide less cover. This can make it difficult for the angler to

induce strikes because circumstances do not allow the fish to seek water from which they would retain a more aggressive posture. I have encountered this problem repeatedly on a tributary of a small Oregon coastal stream. Instead of working their way into the miniature riffles, the lethargic steelhead stay exposed in slower water when the water temperature is in the thirties. Their sense of vulnerability puts them off the bite.

In the 40° to 43° range, steelhead react to various river heights much as they do in the lower temperature range but with a greater tendency to hold closer to the head of the pool. This helps our efforts on small streams or on streams that receive heavy pressure. A steelhead that lies in heavy chop or turbulent riffles toward the head of a pool has a sense of safety and security that will make him vulnerable to our offerings.

In the 44° to 49° range, higher water tends to put fish at tailout sections, at lower-drift sections, or at any spot that offers the proper depth and flow. Thus, you may find steelhead in places that are utterly ridiculous to fish when rivers are at their normal levels. *A steelhead is always trying to seek a certain flow, given its metabolism.* Lower-drift and tailout sections often have the right combination. The upper part of the drift and the head of the pool are usually too fast or turbulent in the high water. This, however, is relative. In a smaller pool of a river divided into two forks by an island, the head of the pool may be just perfect.

As water clears, steelhead move into the drift. This is probably the most common circumstance under which winter steelhead are angled for in the Northwest. This fact alone gets steelheaders into trouble. I'll explain. In the Northwest, anglers use daily published river height (river stage) readings to determine when a river is fishable. The hordes usually begin converging on a stream when it comes close to its ideal height. Since most of their efforts are concentrated when the river is at a particular height, they become set in their approach, always fishing the river in the exact same way. If they happen to fish the river when it is above or below ideal height, they most always come away complaining that a new freshet is needed to bring in new fish or that the river is too high.

When fishing in water 44° to 49° with river receding to low winter levels, steelhead will be most negotiable in water that has a *broken surface*. In these conditions, search for steelhead in riffles and chop to be found at the head of pools. Tailout and "lower-drift" fishing is practically worthless in such circumstances unless spawned-out steelhead are present.

I think it is important to mention at this point that the above discussion should serve only as a framework for you to use in your approach but *not* as an end-all answer. Some aspects of fishing are very easily described. It is simple to suggest the use of a particular hook or blade. But how do I describe what a river looks like when it is clearing? How could I describe steelhead water that is the right speed and depth? I can't and to try would ultimately end in your confusion and lost interest. There is simply no substitute for stream experience! Being on the river will give you much more than I or anyone else could ever offer in a book. If you are new to steelheading, many of the points I make, especially those concerning environmental relationships, will only take on meaning with experience.

Spinners for steelhead, salmon and trout. See Chapter 14 for an in-depth discussion of when to use these spinners and for what species.

Trout Standard

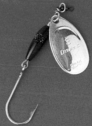

Ed's Pregnant

McKenzie Medium

Black Mallard

Summer Green

McKenzie Dark

Inside blade tape placement

broad
French blade

narrow
French blade

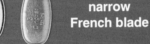

Different body weights for different conditions

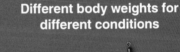

Asa Pearl's Special

Winter Steelhead Standard

Green Standard

Chartreuse Standard

Columbia Gorge

Black and Black

A spawned out steelhead is guided close to shore. The fish hit Asa Pearl's Special. Fish like this have no food value and should be released. Asa Pearl photo

Here the author plays an active coho taken from a deep hole in low water. Coho quickly race upstream but often become trapped in deep holes if the water falls quickly. David Davis photo

The author hoists a 23-lb. toolie chinook taken from the Little Manistee. All Michigan chinook are the toolie strain so they darken up rather quickly upon entering a river and most should be released. Sheldon Cohen photo

While fishing for salmon on the North Umpqua, the author latched onto this late summer steelhead and jack salmon. Jed Davis photo

A nice winter-run taken after a rare Oregon snowfall. The water was 37° and a gaudy No. 5 silver-plate did the trick. Sheldon Cohen photo

Steve Trask with a fine late winter-run. The fish was taken in March on the Alsea River. Jed Davis photo

This 15½-lb. steelhead took a spinner in riffly 48° water. Jed Davis photo

Fallbacks and Confusion

The above discussion, or for that matter any discussion in this book, is focused on angling for pre-spawning steelhead — that is, fresh steelhead that have recently entered the river and are striving to reach their spawning grounds. Anyone who has caught winter steelhead from mid-season on knows that, as the season progresses, increasing numbers of spawned-out steelhead will be encountered. These are fish that have accomplished their task, preparing the way for future generations of steelhead that will once again ascend the rivers. These fish have a host of nicknames — fallbacks, snakes, re-runs, comebacks. They are distinguished by their dark spawning colors, caved-in bellies, and skinny appearances. Oftentimes, these fish will shed their spawning colors and take on a pre-spawning silver color. Although it will be slightly more gray-silver than a fresh steelhead's chrome-silver, these fish are sometimes mistaken for fresh steelhead. The angler proudly fillets his catch only to discover white, mushy flesh that is worthless table-fare. The true identity of silver fallbacks is given away by a head that appears disproportionately large to its body or by an inflamed anal opening, characteristic of post-spawning salmonids.

When the spawning ritual has been completed, steelhead begin to work their way downstream. Biological changes allow them to once again feed. If successful in finding adequate nutrition and overcoming extreme exhaustion, they may survive the ordeal and once again return to the stream the following year as robust steelhead.

I see no harm in fishing for fallbacks as long as they are all released. Killing one to show a friend or drowning one in a heavy fish batter so as to obscure the taste is a waste of a potential resource that could be of benefit in the future. Only up to ten percent of all Northwest fallbacks ever survive, but the precious few who do make it carry the genes of a hearty fish that is capable of generating others like it. In the Great Lakes, Dr. Robert Behnke, in *Trout* magazine reports that 20 to 50 percent of fallbacks survive the ordeal. It is for this reason that sportsmen should release all spawned-out steelhead. I feel a wonderful sense of pride and accomplishment when I release a fallback. It is as if I am helping out a friend.

In regard to behavior, one must not confuse fallbacks with fresh steelhead. Fallbacks have slightly different behavior patterns. For one, they love to hold in shallow tail-outs, regardless of water temperature and river height. In fact, they will hold right in the break. Second, these fish will also hold in deep pools with a current too slow for fresh steelhead.

The point is this: If during February and March you have great success on fallbacks in slack pools and shallow breaks, don't expect to return the following November and find the steelhead in the same spots. In most cases, you won't.

The Key to Winter Steelhead Success

There are a number of things that the steelheader should pay careful attention to when pursuing winter-runs with spinners. These are simple considerations and, yet, they can be so instrumental in achieving consistent success.

In Chapter 2, I stressed the importance of getting away from the save-the-spinner syndrome. If you start fishing the spinner to save the spinner, instead of fishing the spinner

to reach the fish, your effectiveness is doing to go way down. You have to accept the idea that you are going to lose an average of two to four spinners per day if you are to be fishing correctly. The point I wish to make is that you should always carry at least eight spinners of your "bread-and-butter" spinner to the river. It will be rare that you lose eight in one day, but not five or six. You need to have enough spinners on hand so that you are beyond worrying about using them all up. In this way, you will be psychologically freed from the fear of having nothing to fish with. The result is that you will fish the lure to the best of your ability all day long.

When pursuing winter-runs, always concentrate on working the spinner blade and the spinner as a whole as slowly as possible. As discussed earlier, the slow-spinning blade gives off stronger visual pulsations and flash that will better induce steelhead into striking. A slow-moving spinner also presents more flash and gaudiness for a greater period of time. A typical winter steelhead with slow metabolism may be inclined to strike if the lure is presented for a greater period of time. Mind you, it is not the slowness of the lure per se that is attracting the fish. Rather, it is the slowness of the fish's decision to strike that creates the need for a slow retrieval — that is, if a spinner is placed close enough to the fish for a longer period of time, his slowed-down aggressive instincts will have enough time to reach a threshold of excitement which will cause the fish to take action and strike. Once the winter-run has made that decision to strike, even 33° water will not prevent him from swimming quickly to intercept a spinner. *It is getting him to make that initial move that is the difficult part.* A slow-blade spin and a slow-moving spinner optimize the chances of exciting winter-runs to the point where they initiate a response to strike.

When you fish a new section of a stream, especially if it is a small stream, fish everything initially . . . *everything.* Fish every nook-and-cranny. Leave no water uncovered. As I pointed out in an earlier section, steelhead hold in different types of waters and this varies according to the various environmental conditions. You will discover that certain spots that seem marginal, and which are otherwise unfishable with drift gear and plugs, consistently hold steelhead. This may involve a lot of initial tedious exploration because it will take a long time to work your way through a drift. But, after you have been through it five or ten times, you will begin to discover where the fish are and where they "ain't." Small streams can often be surprisingly deceiving. I have discovered some fantastic holes that most "know-it-alls" would pass up with a sigh of confidence.

During the course of any year, I will share my experiences with other anglers. I suppose that my enthusiasm conveys a feeling of success and satisfaction because I am always asked the same question by winter steelhead anglers who want to make good of their precious fishing time: "What's the secret?" There really are no secrets per se. I know of no secret holes that hold dozens of steelhead and I have no secret spinners or techniques not shared in this book. I think that if there is one thing that has greatly augmented my success and increased my satisfaction, it is that I know how to identify and I know where to look for the best steelhead spinner water. I truly believe that a good many steelheaders who are now drift fishing and pulling plugs would rather throw spinners but quickly become discouraged. Why? It is because they try to fish the spinners in the same runs, on the same rivers that everyone else goes to. They are fishing spinners but they are *seeing* the river and fishing it as would a Corky and Egger. And the one thing that is going to make the difference between erratic results and consistent success is your ability to know what water is right for steelhead spinner fishing and then to opportunistically take advantage of the versatility of the spinner in a way not possible with the more popular drift and plug methods. Just as it is essential to free yourself from the save-the-spinner syndrome, it is equally as important to throw out the drift-fishing mentality that limits steelhead fishing to a small portion of the river and only on certain drifts. You have to start seeing the river differently. How does one do that?

Have you ever crossed a section of a river, or passed by a smaller-sized river, or come across a seldom-fished river, and then asked yourself, "Why doesn't anyone fish that?" Ask around. Eventually you will find out why and, in general, it's not because there are no steelhead. You will hear things like, "It's really snaggy in there," or "Not many good drifts," or "Too shallow, drifts are really short," or "Fish don't hit up there," or "Can't position my boat right," or "Lots of logs that steelhead hide under, can't get to them." What these statements are is a collection of frustrations, voiced by drifters or plug-pullers who couldn't fish the water properly. This does not mean that there is something wrong with drift gear or plugs. What it does mean is that techniques were not matched to the water; hence, the vast majority of anglers who fish these popular methods never return to these waters. These are precisely the types of waters that are tailor-made for spinners because spinners don't have to bump along the bottom as do pencil lead and split shot. In order for drift gear to work properly, a drift of minimal length is needed. Not for spinners. You can plop your hardware into a 5-foot by 5-foot hole and fish that hole with total effectiveness. Boat positioning is needed to fish drift gear properly. You can't drift fish directly upstream or downstream very well. This is not the case with spinners. You can throw anywhere and everywhere from any position. Steelhead, especially in Michigan, will lie under logs that never get flushed downstream. Since drift bobbers and eggs must pass close to a steelhead in order for him to take, it is often difficult, if not impossible, to fish this terminal tackle. If you can get within ten feet with a flashy spinner, those steelhead can be enticed to move great distances to strike.

Ninety percent of the steelhead I catch come from upper river, tiny river, and seldom-fished areas. I call these places "rivers with glass slippers." When I explore a new river, I explore as much of it as is driftable or walkable. In other words, I do the whole thing. I know what I am looking for — small pockets, pools, riffles, logs, and terraces. I am looking for highly-defined water, water in which the bottom contour is given away by what I observe on the surface. I know that my spinners have limitations. Classic fast and deep runs may hold a lot of fish but are best covered by bottom bouncers. Better to leave this water to the drifters and plug-pullers. And they reciprocate by showing little interest in my water, the sight of which gives me goose bumps and makes my heart pound. Good steelhead spinner fishermen are seldom seen and this will always be the case until such a time that their numbers greatly increase. This

is because they often seek out waters which the vast majority of anglers have found to be difficult to fish.

There are no books, maps, or indexes that will tell you where these spinner meccas are. Your own personal effort and perseverance is the key that will unlock the treasure of spinner waters. You simply have to get in the car and drive, explore, and take notes. You would be surprised at what is available. A careful eye will uncover seldom-used boat launches, obscure paths, and places where a boat can easily be dumped off the side of a road. As I said, there are no secret documents that will unleash a myriad of productive waters. However, there is one source for Oregonians and Washingtonians that will give you some clue as to which rivers are worth the effort of serious exploration. In each of these states, anglers are required to record on a punch card each steelhead and salmon that is caught and harvested. At the end of the season, the statistics are compiled and made available to the public. *Salmon Trout Steelheader* magazine published these statistics for three or four years in their annual winter steelhead issue but stopped with the 1982 issue. Frank Amato Publications has published a booklet entitled "Steelhead and Salmon Sport Catch Statistics for Oregon, 1971-1980." This publication is a good source and if not available, one should contact Richard L. Berry at the Oregon Department of Fish and Wildlife.

The publishing of these data can be extremely helpful to the steelhead spinner angler . . . if you know what to look for. The tendency of most anglers is to check out where the most steelhead have been traditionally caught and then head for these rivers. I purposely stay away from these rivers. If thousands of steelhead are being caught, thousands of anglers are going after them. I look for streams where small numbers of steelhead are caught but which nonetheless consistently produce these small numbers of steelhead from year to year. If I take note of one of these streams and see that it has sections that are good spinner prospects, chances are I've found myself a river. My favorite winter steelhead stream in Oregon cranks out a "whopping" 120 steelhead per year and, yet, I have never skunked on this river, even in bad years. I had some memorable four-, five-, and six-fish days. Sounds contradictory, doesn't it? Why the disparity? That's easy. I drive just a bit farther than most people will. The stream is small, snaggy, well-defined, and nearly impossible to fish with drift gear. There is also no room to run Wee-Warts. The result is that few, very few, people ever fish it. Although the run of steelhead never seems to be more than a few hundred, I am just about the only person who seriously fishes this stream. Think about it. I fish this stream with a method that allows me to search out every inch of river and I hit every spot fresh. The result is that I do well.

However, I would like to offer a bit of advice. Should you be motivated by the above discussion such that you eventually come upon a small stream that produces good angling, your ticket to year-in/year-out action will be enhanced by the respect you show for the stream. By releasing most of the steelhead that you catch, you can enjoy the resource without taxing the steelhead's ability to regenerate itself. Thus, you will ensure that future generations of steelhead are once again able to return to the river to spawn. The steelhead will benefit and so will you! By keeping everything you catch, you will slowly be digging your own grave . . . and the steelhead's, too.

A number of anglers won't tell anyone where they fish because they fear that someone will steal all available fish. I don't tell people where I fish, but for different reasons. First, I seek out obscure rivers, in part, because I want to be left alone. Only occasionally do I fish with a partner and even when alone, I hate to see other boats. I don't care how many steelhead a river cranks out. If the day ever comes where I can't find a stream that offers solitude for the better part of the day, I think I will give up steelhead fishing. My second reason for not divulging my drifts is due to the catch-and-kill-harvest-anything mentality which is still sadly embedded in the minds of the great majority of steelheaders. My most prized streams are delicate little gems that could not stand the stampede of callous individuals — those little men with big egos and greedy hands who are indulged in the salvation of their fragile masculinities. These pathetic souls would see a delicate little stream, just as they see everything else in the outdoors, as being present for their exclusive enjoyment and exploitation. They would rake the river, taking anything and everything. And if the fishing starts to go down hill, they would be quick to put the blame on some institution or minority group, never realizing, never considering that it was *they* who might have had something to do with the stream's demise. This is precisely why I don't tell people where I fish. Better to let these hungry rats crawl over each other at some roadside armpit where the Department of Fish and Wildlife feeds them yearly rations of brood trout.

Winter Steelhead Spinners

Unfortunately, most discussions of technique start with a consideration of what the best bait is. From my point of view, an understanding of steelhead behavior and the development of an optimal presentation far outweighs the use of one spinner versus another. Put the expert and the amateur on the same stream. Give the amateur the finest silver-plated winter steelhead spinners, and give the expert some tarnished brass spinners. The expert will outfish the amateur by a margin of at least three to one. When it comes to winter steelhead, a good technique can overcome the disadvantage of a less-than-optimal spinner, but I've never seen a good spinner make up for a lack of technique or knowledge.

Selecting spinners for winter-runs is relatively easy. We need spinners that are large, flashy, well-weighted, and with specifically colored adornments. Let's first take a look at homemade spinners and then turn our attention to commercially-offered spinners.

The best winter steelhead spinners, those used in 90 percent of all winter steelhead conditions, have four qualities: weight, maximum flash, size, fluorescent adornments. A No. 5 winter steelhead spinner (most commonly used by experts) should weigh close to or slightly over half an ounce when completed. A No. 4 should weigh somewhere around a third of an ounce. If in construction, you can get away with using a heavier body that increases weight without reducing blade responsiveness, this is desirable although not always necessary. I use No. 5s for most of my winter fishing and I have never felt a need to have a spinner that weighed more than half an ounce. A lot of people like to use worm weights with their No. 5s, the result being a three-

quarter-ounce spinner. I shy away from the use of such lures because they work the water with less finesse. They aren't as fun to fish. I also find that, if one is skilled in presenting the spinner, working a lighter spinner through a very deep hole can be done quite effectively. Here again, I must emphasize the greater importance of skill over spinner. A No. 5 spinner that employs a heavy worm weight is often a crutch against the angler's lack of skill.

Frank Amato happily explains to a group of steelheaders how he'd like to be buried next to the Deschutes River. Jed Davis photo

Maximum flash allows the spinner to be seen over a greater periphery, thereby attracting and exciting low-metabolismed steelhead from greater distances. This is especially desirable for winter steelheading because the volume of river water is greater and maximum underwater visibility is seldom present except in long-term drying trends and on small streams. Standard nickel is preferred over brass and copper. The best finish, however, is genuine silver which will reflect most of the light that hits it, thus rendering a strong flash. Nickel, although silver-like in appearance, absorbs a good portion of the light that hits it and will give off a gray-silver or almost-black flash. The finest spinner has a silver-plated blade and silver-plated body. A silver body, in concert with silver blade, gives off a flash that cannot be matched by any other combination of materials. I have been using this type of winter steelhead spinner for years and have yet to find anything that comes close to matching it if my goal is maximum flash. A lot of anglers like to use a silver-plated blade and a fluorescent body painted red or yellow. This is fine but, if I had to make a choice, I would rather fish a spinner with a nickel blade and body versus a spinner with a silver blade and fluorescent-painted body.

Large, gaudy spinners are very effective in exciting steelhead with low metabolism. A No. 5 with silver-plated blade and body did this Michigan steelhead in. The fish bit in 32-degree water. Sheldon Cohen photo

In terms of size, bigger spinners are more visible to the fish and attract the most attention from a greater periphery. There will be few instances that do not warrant the use of a No. 4 or No. 5 . . . this you can be sure of! In typical winter conditions, a No. 5 will be the best size to use 80 percent of the time. Some people feel more comfortable with No. 4s. They will work nearly as well as No. 5s but there will be limitations in the amount of depth that can be attained. This is why I advise the use of No. 5s. However, always keep a few No. 2s and No. 3s handy for those tiny streams that get low and clear or for conditions where fish are being constantly spooked.

The finest spinners have a piece of brightly-colored tubing on the shank and the same or very similarly-colored pressure-sensitive tape placed on the *inside* (see Chapter 3) of the blade. Don't mix colors. If you are using red tubing, use a red tape. The best all-around colors for winter steelhead are the fluorescents: orange, fire orange (red-orange), or bright red. My personal favorite is fire orange. Fluorescent yellows and chartreuse are good very early in the season but seem to lose effectiveness by early December. Greens and blues are not used to any great degree. However, black tape and tubing can be very effective on some streams. I fish one stream here in Oregon where for some unknown reason, my silver-plated spinners with black adornments put my silver and fire-orange spinners to utter shame. I am still trying to figure this one out.

The subject of "the best" spinner one can buy always raises the emotions of anglers quick to defend their lures with photo albums and countless stories. I always say, "Fish with what you have confidence in." I personally have no use for Rooster Tails, Panther Martins, or Luhr Jensen Metrics and Steelhead Spinners. Each has problems and limitations which would not allow me to pursue my technique as outlined in this book. However, if you have con-

fidence in any one of these, I will be the last one to discourage you. With this in mind, let's proceed.

"Bud's Steelhead Spinner" has been around the Northwest for a long time. It is a quality, economy spinner that possesses some admirable features: 1) It has a .026-in. French blade and 2) weighted body; in addition, 3) all models have quality shank tubing; I like it because 4) the blade spins dependably and it's designed in such a way so as to minimize spinner wobble; finally, 5) the price is very attractive. The features I don't like are: 1) The style hook — a lot of fish will be lost when they strike; 2) hook sizes are too small for the larger-sized spinners; 3) although weighted, they are not weighted enough. Still, this lure is a favorite among Northwest steelheaders. It's a decent spinner but by no means the tool of an expert.

Luhr Jensen's Metrics and Steelhead Spinners are an imitation of Bud's. Both are marketed as economy spinners. Both have qualities which from my standpoint are intolerable. In addition to the points mentioned about Bud's, I would add the following. First, the shank tubing used is awful. It is dull in color and gives a faded appearance. On the Metric, no tubing is used on the treble. Second, the wrong clevis size is used on the large steelhead models. This will result in greater resistance and more spinner wobble. A different style French blade is employed that differs noticably from the other models. I call it a "fat French." The latter has bad connotations but that is just as well. Although the blade has more surface area than would be found on a standard French, this is done at the expense of a spinner that produces too much resistance. A variety of Steelhead Spinners are offered with painted blades and bodies. Spinners are available in green, blue, and fluorescent orange. They may look appealing but from my point of view, they defeat the purpose of a winter steelhead spinner. The greatest flash is produced with bright metallic surfaces, not with dark greens and blues. On the positive side, I do like the weight and size of the No. 5 and No. 7 Metrics. Although the No. 7 is larger than my bread-and-butter No. 5s, this spinner is nonetheless very close to what I use. However, in terms of flash, gaudiness, and versatility, it doesn't hold a candle to my No. 5s with a silver-plated blade and body, and with fluorescent adornments. If your concern is price, the price of the Steelhead Spinners is very attractive.

Mepps' spinners are the world's most popular lure. Their introduction of the spinner with its French blade has had a tremendous impact on fishing worldwide. In terms of steelhead, their popularity has faded considerably in recent years as companies more interested in the small steelhead market have surged ahead. The advantages of Mepps Aglia are: 1) extremely well-balanced blade that spins smoothly and on command with a minimum of spinner wobble, 2) available with silver-plated blade, 3) proper style round-bend treble, 4) quality red-shank tubing. The disadvantages are that: 1) it's overpriced, 2) it's underweighted, 3) its round-bend treble on popular No. 4 size is one size too small. Mepps is a quality lure but I am not so sure I would want to lose two to four per day at $2.00 apiece. If you choose Mepps, the best steelhead models are those that employ a red/yellow body and a silver blade. Bucktails and squirrel-tails are not suited for winter steelhead fishing because they are void of flash or bright color.

The Smolt was introduced by Quality Tackle in 1982,

and has already gained wide acceptance in the Northwest. It is the first spinner ever developed that employs a French-type blade with a worm weight. Its strong points are: 1) silver-plated blade, 2) superior VMC round-treble hook with red tubing, 3) maximum weight for working lure deeply, 4) can be cast a very long distance due to worm weight. Two aspects of the spinner concern me: 1) Smolt employs an .018-in. blade which means that pulsations on the rod tip will be more difficult to read; 2) considerable spinner wobble is produced because three-fourths of the body is lead, and one-fourth of the body is plastic beads (see Chapter 3, "Avoiding Spinner Wobble"). Still, this is a good spinner, designed specifically for steelhead, that should be considered by anyone who prefers to buy instead of build.

The Blue Fox Vibrax is another relative newcomer. The manufacturer claims that the lure emits superior sonic attraction. This may be so. However, *all* spinners give off some underwater sound. The lure's strong point is that it has a silver-plated French-type blade and a silver-plated body. This gives the lure superior visibility. Its disadvantages are: 1) no tubing on shank, 2) *highly* underweighted. This latter point disqualifies it as a steelhead spinner.

The above spinners represent the class of spinners that employ the preferred French blade. It has always been my feeling that it is the French-type blade that can be fished most effectively due to its versatility at all speeds plus the ability of the angler to control the speed of the blade via pulsations on the rod tip. However, there are spinners that employ different style blades. Two deserve mention.

The Rooster Tail by Yakima Bait Company has been around for some 20 years. The spinner is known to just about anyone who ever picked up a spinning rod. The cosmetic design is appealing and the availability of colors is impressive. What's more, the swing blade is silver-plated on appropriate models. Quality of construction is excellent and, yet, I would never fish a Rooster Tail. Why? Ask anyone who has ever fished one. The clevis is often too-closely sandwiched between the body and eye. Friction from the clevis rubbing against the adjacent parts means that the clevis cannot swing freely. Add this concern to a relatively unresponsive swing blade in tandem with a friction-provoking folded clevis, and you have one lure that is difficult to fish because there is always a problem with getting the blade to start spinning. If the folks at Yakima Bait had left a greater space for a stirrup clevis and added the appropriate French-type blade, they would probably have sold many more Rooster Tails over the years. Experts will simply not tolerate such an unpredictable lure.

The Panther Martin, manufactured by Harrison-Hoge, has a wide following among anglers. The spinner blade fits directly on the shaft, always keeping the blade at the same angle. While the blade functions adequately, the same degree of control and manipulation that the angler exercises over a well-designed French-bladed spinner is lacking. In my opinion, a stronger current is needed to get the Panther Martin working and to keep it working. The slow-blade spin that is so effective on steelhead is harder to achieve with a Panther

Martin. While the design is interesting and the spinner certainly works, I feel that overall, it is a less versatile blade to work with when compared to the French-type blade. One strong point in the Panther Martin's favor is the well-designed lead body which beautifully complements each respective

Denny Partridge, well-known Rogue River guide, with two winter steelhead from an Oregon coastal stream. Jed Davis photo

blade size. The lure is heavy, yet compact, which means it can be cast far and worked deeply. While the paint finish on the lead is very durable, the quality of the colors in terms of brightness and richness leaves much to be desired. Finally, I am not aware of any models that have tubing on the hook shank. However, it must be said that models with silver-plated blades are available.

It is quite evident from the above discussion that I have reservations about every commercially-offered spinner. This is one reason why I make my own. As you further develop your spinner technique, you will begin to develop certain preferences and realize that you need a special design to match your needs. Building your own may become very attractive.

Chapter 8

Summer Steelhead

STRONG RAYS OF SUNSHINE ILLUMINATED the clear, cool river and its brownish pebbles, while crinkling sounds of water in shallow riffles pacified my soul. The wide, shallow flats of the McKenzie River extended downstream for at least a half-mile. A No. 2 spinner was gently cast behind a rock. I watched closely but the spinner was lost in the 18 inches of white, choppy froth. A broad silver flash appeared and was quickly followed by a streaking form that walked the water's surface in search of freedom. This is a thrill I experience over and over again, one that leaves me in awe. Why does a ten-pound fish hold in 18 inches of water on a hot, sunny day and then strike a small lure with a ferocity that contradicts its usual behavior? No one can ever know for sure. What we do know is that this is part of the incredible world of summer steelhead.

Summer steelheading is a sport all its own. The ambience, environment, and tools used to outsmart these "Gifts of Summer" are in strong contrast to our winter steelhead experience. For this reason, it is wise to leave a winter steelhead mentality where it belongs . . . with winter steelhead.

For summer, circumstances cause us to form a new set of rules. And it is very important that we remain flexible. Just as I stressed the importance of learning to see a winter steelhead river in terms of spinner fishing versus seeing it for drift fishing, I feel that it is equally important to see a summer river exclusively in terms of summer-runs. To do this, we must psychologically free ourselves from winter steelhead technique. More often than not, it simply does not apply to summer-runs. But I want to stress that it is not that summer-runs are different from winter-runs. They aren't! All steelhead, save east of the Cascades strains, react similarly given the same temperature range. *It is the different environmental conditions that cause summer-runs to take on a different personality.*

In this chapter, we make a close study of summer steelhead. Once again, effective fishing must start with a consideration of the environment. One of the most difficult challenges of summer steelhead fishing is finding the fish. If we know what type of water they are in search of, then catching them on a consistent basis becomes much easier.

The Upstream Journey

The first of the year's summer-runs start trickling in as early as January. However, so few enter our rivers at this time that it is almost ridiculous to try and fish for them. By April, the run starts to get into full swing. Depending on the river, the peak can occur anywhere from early June to November. For example, Southwest Washington fish peak during the latter part of June, whereas McKenzie steelheading is best in August. Deschutes and North Umpqua steelheading is very good in September. Much of this is dependent upon how far steelhead must travel . . . but not always. Rogue River and North Umpqua steelhead have a relatively short journey but are simply late-returning steelhead.

The main difference in the migration of summer and winter steelhead is that with summer-runs, there is relatively little fluctuation in the environmental conditions that are part of a typical summer steelhead stream. Whether in Oregon or Michigan, the precipitation that falls during the late spring and summer has little influence on river level and clarity. Streams consistently run at the same level for a three- or four-month period. The result is that summer-runs will be travelling in very similar conditions all summer long. Because a minimum water temperature of 40° is needed for steelhead migration, we can then always assume that summer steelhead will not be stopped because of water temperature because it is rare that summer streams will be 40° or below.

So what are the factors that determine whether a summer-run

will move or will not move? Two factors seem to have the greatest influence. First is available lighting. While summer-runs can be seen jumping Shearer Falls on the Deschutes in broad daylight, I would say that for safety reasons, summer steelhead prefer to migrate under the cover of shadows, clouds, or at night. The counting station at Winchester Dam on Oregon's North Umpqua gives credence to this view. During a sunny day, one typically sees stragglers through the viewing station's large glass windows. At dusk, however, large numbers of fish can be seen congregating in the man-made pools of the counting station.

The second factor would be water temperature. When considering winter migration, we tend to think in terms of minimum water temperature needed for migration. With summer-runs, we look to maximum water temperature. What I mean here is that we are not concerned with minimum water temperature because none of our summer rivers have a temperature of $40°$ or below. But, at times, temperatures do climb into the sixties and seventies, especially on streams like the East Fork Lewis and Washougal. Coastal strains of steelhead from west of the Cascades will migrate freely when temperatures are below $60° - 62°$. Temperatures above this range cause the fish to become lethargic. They will hibernate in deep holes until a favorable weather change lowers water temperatures into the high fifties. With steelhead strains originating from east of the Cascades, the tolerance is higher. From an evolutionary/environmental point of view, it has to be because of the scorching summer conditions of the eastern plain. These steelhead will migrate in waters up to the high sixties or even $70°$. This fact amazes me. I think of steelhead as being cold-water fish. Thinking that they comfortably migrate and strike lures in $70°$ seems to be very strange.

Interim — East, West, Off-Colored?!

The section that follows, "The Core: Sunlight, Water Temperature, Holding Water, and Spinner Selection," is the very heart of this chapter. Yet, it only applies to strains of summer steelhead that are found west of the Cascades. (Great Lakes summer-runs are among this "west of the Cascades" group). Eastern summer steelhead found in rivers like the Deschutes, Methow, and Grand Ronde are a different type of steelhead altogether, more closely related to the desert "Red Band" trout than they are to the Western Oregon and Washington State summer-runs. The main difference, as mentioned, centers around tolerance for warmer temperatures.

Whereas a western Cascade summer-run becomes lethargic at $60°$ to $65°$, a desert summer-run will do well up to $70°$ or even $75°$. This means that spinner strategy will need to be adjusted for this eastern strain of fish. But just as desert steelhead have different tolerances when compared to coastal strains, there are also differences among coastal strains. Skamania summer-runs should not be equated with North Umpqua, Siletz, or Rogue River strains. I have taken summer-runs in good numbers when the North Umpqua was $67°$! Sixty-seven degrees on the McKenzie would send the Skamanias to a deep hole where they would remain motionless until the water cooled. The point is that each strain of summer-runs must be treated individually. Sixty-five degrees on the Siletz and $65°$ on the South Santiam does not necessarily dictate the same strategy.

Another factor not considered in the following section is water clarity. The findings and recommendations work on the premise that the stream you are fishing is gin-clear. Most steelhead streams do run clear in the summer . . . but not all. The one I am most familiar with is the South Santiam. As alluded to in an earlier chapter, monmerlite clay runs into Green Peter Reservoir. Instead of settling, it remains suspended in the water. This same water eventually flows into the South Santiam giving this stream an off-colored cast for the entire season. Even though the South Santiam gets the exact same strain of steelhead from the same hatchery that the nearby McKenzie gets, spinner strategy is different on both streams. The off-colored cast of the "South" allows fish to feel more secure because less direct sunlight penetrates the off-colored water. Where a No. 3 brass in $54°$ to $57°$ and in direct sunlight would spook McKenzie fish, the same lure will do quite nicely on the Santiam. The point is this: Summer steelhead will have varying dispositions depending on water clarity. This means that spinner strategy must be altered.

The Deschutes is another example of a river, along with other rivers, that runs off-colored during the summer but to discuss every particular river, every set of conditions, and then recommend spinners for each, is beyond the scope of this book. Therefore, I have selected the most typical situation — a low, gin-clear coastal strain river. The points I outline below will be relevant to this general set of conditions. Please remember though that, should you ever find yourself exploring an off-colored stream and/or Eastern Washington/Oregon stream, two basic rules will apply: First, desert steelhead will have a greater tolerance for warmer water flows. This means that large gaudy spinners can be used in warmer waters and that steelhead will become lethargic at a higher water temperature. Second, off-colored water will give steelhead an added measure of security. This means that large spinners can be used. However, in gin-clear water, these same lures would be totally ineffective.

The Core: Sunlight, Water Temperature, Holding Water, and Spinner Selection

With summer rivers that, for the most part, maintain a consistent level and clarity, it would appear that fishing the spinner for summer-runs may be less complicated relative to winter fishing. Just the opposite is the case. Within the temperature range of $33°$ to $48°$, spinner selection does not alter significantly. Ninety-five percent of my winter-runs come on one size and color spinner. With summer-runs, typically caught in temperatures above $50°$, varying temperatures will dictate the use of different sizes and colors. Then there is the question of lighting. This also has a significant effect on the steelhead's disposition and what it will strike relative to its disposition. Therefore, it is my feeling that in order to be successful on a consistent basis, the steelheader has to constantly be aware of the interplay of water temperature and available lighting. Let's take a look at both factors and then see how this translates into spinner selection.

I like to divide the $50°$ to $62°$ summer steelhead temperature range into four categories: $50°$ to $53°$, $54°$ to $57°$, $58°$ to $61°$, and $62°$ to $65°$. Within each range, steelhead disposition changes. Available lighting will also have a varying effect within each range.

In the 50° to 53° range, I characterize steelhead behavior as being somewhat transitional. The transition is thought of in several respects. First, steelhead will show no preference for a particular type of holding water. This is especially true for 50° and 51°. They can be found in water preferred by winter-runs with lower metabolism. That is, they can be found in the deeper, medium-speed water that winter steelhead gravitate to. But they also can be found in fast, shallow riffles and slick, smooth tailouts. The key here is to fish everything, especially early in the spring when river flows have not receded to their very low levels. As the season progresses, however, I ignore the winter-type waters. Why?

As I angle for summer-runs more and more each year, I have come to believe that the steelhead shows signs of a "river memory" or "habit" that influences their behavior. Simply, a fish that has held in the shallow riffles for six weeks or two months will have a tendency to seek out these types of waters, even if the water temperature drops into a lower range. My experiences on the McKenzie, South Santiam, and North Umpqua rivers demonstrate the point. Early in the season when fishing the 50° to 53° range, I will connect with fresh summer-runs in some of the slower, deeper winter steelhead type waters. As the season progresses, fewer and fewer are to be found in these areas even if the temperature drops down to 50° to 53°. By the latter part of the season, forget it. However, the few that I have taken from these areas late in the season were very fresh, late-returning summer-runs. Furthermore, and most interestingly, if I am fishing late in the season and the water temperature drops to 49°, 50°, or 51°, I will still negotiate the greater majority of my fish in the shallow, riffly waters.

The author hoists his 14-foot Koffler onto the trailer after a day on the McKenzie. He uses the motorized bike to pick up his rig at the end of the drift. David Davis photo

Sunlight begins to have its effect in the 50° to 53° range and this, in turn, has a direct influence on spinner selection. Sunlight is a threat to the steelhead's safety. Anytime you see a rising sun hit the water or the clearing of clouds or fog, you can be certain that summer steelhead will be just a bit more wary, spooky, and less secure. The appearance of any foreign object in their path — if too large, gaudy, or noisy — is going to cause them to either flee in fear or become passive. Our goal is to present a spinner that they will notice and take interest in but which will not spook them. As I discussed in Chapter 1, our goal is to seek the threshold of attraction. This is the name of the game.

What spinners should you use? In the 50° to 53° range, at dawn or dusk or under cloudy conditions, summer-runs will be more "winter-run" oriented than when it is sunny. Under these conditions, one can use some of the larger spinners used for winter-runs and achieve good results. The No. 4 spinner is probably the most popular winter-run spinner. They will work well in this case. My personal choice is a No. 3 spinner. I can do well with No. 4s but I do better with No. 3s. Will No. 5s work? Yes, but because the water is often clear, shallower, and slower, I feel that they are not needed and may in fact spook steelhead.

When the water temperature is at 50° or 51°, the emergence of a bright sun will not cause me to switch from a No. 3. But when the mercury hits 52° or 53°, I find that the No. 3 is too large and gaudy and the fish will not hit it. This is the time to go down to a No. 2 spinner. One of *the* reasons that summer steelheaders continually have very poor luck after 9:00 a.m. and until evening shadows arrive is because they do not make an accommodation to the summer-run's changed environment. Using a large No. 3 or No. 4 spinner on a sunny, clear river in shallow riffles is pointless. You might as well fill your bathtub with water and fish there. Steelhead change personalities in direct sunlight and the only way you can get them to maintain an aggressive posture is by going small, dull, and dark! This means using small No. 0, No. 1, and No. 2 spinners void of fluorescent beads and finishes placed on the lures to catch the fishermen but which otherwise have no purpose.

At this point in the discussion, I think it is a good time to discuss color and finish of summer steelhead spinners. In terms of finish, I prefer brass blades and bodies on No. 3s and No. 4s. On the smaller spinners, I go with a black oxide blade and brass body. In my opinion, silver plating is too gaudy and flashy. We use silver in the winter for maximum flash and visibility in higher, off-colored waters and to excite the low-metabolismed steelhead into striking. In summer we simply don't need it and, in fact, the brightness will spook fish in many instances. Therefore, I think that silver plating blades for summer use is a waste of time and money. Nickel would be a better choice than silver but I feel that brass or copper is the best choice.

On the smaller No. 0, No. 1 and No. 2 spinners, I always use a brass body but I purposely tarnish the beads or body so that they lose all gloss and shine. This helps insure that steelhead will not spook. Tarnishing is simple. I roll the beads in some dirt and put them in an open can which I set aside for months. For blades, my favorites are black oxide blades. I have these specially plated for me at a commercial plating house. They are not available as spinner parts. However, one can buy Mepps Black Fury spinners and use the black blade. Before I considered having any plated, I used to buy these spinners, remove the blade and put it on my own spinner. In essence, I was paying $1.50 for a single blade but since one loses so few No. 1s and No. 2s, it didn't seem like a lot of money. If you decide to go this route, take off that piece of black tape with the yellow dots. It is worthless and pointless. One may ask, why not simply paint the blades black? As pointed out in Chapter 4, I tried it. In shallow riffles, the blade is constantly knocking against pebbles and rocks. It peels off quite rapidly. Black oxide will last far beyond the life of the spinner.

Brass blades for No. 0, No. 1, and No. 2 spinners also work well if tarnished. Carry them around in your pocket with loose change for a few weeks. They'll tarnish up beautifully. I have been asked whether I think black oxide will outfish the tarnished brass. I am partial to the black but if matched against a good angler, I cannot imagine that I would significantly outfish him because of the blade. As I have said repeatedly: Skill, above everything else, is the key factor!

As with winter steelhead spinners, I never use plastic beads. Outside of human cosmetic appeal, they have no purpose and take up valuable room on the shaft that can be used for additional weighting. That leaves pressure-sensitive tapes and shank tubing. Any of the popular colors will work. I have a strong preference for fluorescent kelly green and dark green, both of which are available in solids and prisms. These, far and away, have been my best colors for all trout and salmon spinners when water temperature is above 50°. Blues can also be effective. I used to use yellows but the greens proved to be far superior for summer-runs on the streams that I fish. I think that oranges and fluorescent reds are okay but not nearly as effective as greens are in the summer (water above 50°). Black is also an effective summer color. This would be my summer steelhead order of preference: green, black, blue, yellow, orange, red, hot pink.

I place tubing on the hook shank of No. 3s and No. 4s only. The smaller-sized spinners are left blank. On the smaller-sized spinners, I place tape on the inside of the blade if using a brass blade. Black blades are usually left blank. As you can imagine, my pet No. 2 with black blade and brass body is very plain in appearance. That's how I like it. It would never sell a retailer or distributor, but it does a good sales job on those summer-runs.

In the 54° to 57° range, summer-runs become very predictable. For one, their preference in water is very clearly defined. While they will rest and strike in smooth, shallow tailouts, they are most negotiable in fast, riffled water of up to three feet. At dawn, dusk, or under cloudy conditions, they can be found in less turbulent water. During these conditions, I tend to think of them as holding in "runs" — that is, water with a good flow that lies downstream from riffles or an upstream obstacle, perhaps slightly riffled, but without any distinct definition other than the water flows at a medium speed. When the sun hits the water, all of this changes. They will seek out the very head of pools and runs where the greatest amount of turbulence exists. In other words, they move right in or under the white, choppy froth. And it need not be deep either. Eleven inches to three feet is fine. They will also move into deep water that has no more than a medium speed but a heavy chop. However, I do not generally fish the latter because it is difficult to get small spinner down to the bottom. I leave this water for the drift fishermen but then they leave the shallows for me. A good relationship!

Another spot summer-runs tend to hold in during sunny conditions is at the edge of drop-offs. These are locations where a shallow, riffled run gradually descends into a deep pool. The steelhead will hold right at the point where the light-brown color of the pebbles and rocks meets the deep green or blue of the pool below. Of all the locations in which I take summer-runs, these are the types of spots that produce the best steelheading. "Sliding tails," as I call them, are overlooked by a great many anglers seeking summer steelhead. In other circumstances, anglers recognize that steelhead may lie in these spots but they approach these hot spots in the wrong way. They reason that, since the sun is out, the steelhead will hold in the deep section of the pool below the confluence of the shallow and deep sections. They commonly start hot-shotting at this point and thereby pass up the chance to run their plugs in front of the steelhead. On many occasions, I have followed three or four boats through a sliding tail with each boat running their plugs through the pool. I will rest the water for ten minutes and then pick off a steelhead on the first cast.

In the darker conditions, the larger No. 3 and No. 4 spinners will work well, although your best best is the No. 3. When the sun hits the water, these spinners become useless pieces of junk. At this point, you must go down to a No. 2 as described above and concentrate on those riffles and sliding tails. This is where the steelhead will be most negotiable. You may ask, "Why would such a big fish be so aggressive in water where they become so vulnerable?" Anytime a steelhead moves into new holding water, he will become more aggressive in the new position. You would think that large six- to 15-pound trout would become very wary in 18 inches of water in direct sunlight but this simply is not the case. Of all conditions in which I pursue winter and summer steelhead, these are the conditions in which I find steelhead to be *the* most aggressive. And wouldn't you think just the opposite? In many cases, it is not a question of them chasing the spinner. They will chase it 25 feet! It's a case of striking as soon as the lure hits the water before the spinner has a chance to start spinning! My initial experiences with this phenomenon make up some of my most precious memories. On one occasion, I hooked and landed three steelhead on three casts. After the second fish, I screamed, "This isn't supposed to happen." By the third fish, I was totally speechless. On another occasion, I negotiated seven steelhead and landed four, all within 35 minutes and in a 50-yard stretch of water. The key of course is knowing where to be and when to be there but, in terms of spinners, always go small, dull, and dark.

Are shallow riffles the only places where sunlight summer-runs go? No! Many will hold in slick tailouts if no riffles are nearby. These fish can be negotiated but not with the same consistency as the riffle steelhead. But this does not mean that it is not worth your effort. Oftentimes, you will be sight-fishing for these fish. If you can see them, they can see you. They will be very wary. There are two methods I use to negotiate them employing a No. 0 or No. 1 spinner. In one situation, I will leave my boat upstream and approach them on foot very slowly and quietly. I will then make continued passes at them sometimes waiting 20 seconds between each pass. The other method involves anchoring upstream from the steelhead I have spotted lying on the break. I anchor directly above the fish. I then swing the spinner down and dangle it in front of the fish's nose. If he doesn't take after a minute, I move on.

In the 58° to 62° range, the same rules apply with the following exceptions. In the darker conditions alluded to above, I never go larger than a No. 3 and I use the No. 3 only in situations where fish are well-protected. Otherwise I use a No. 2. When the sun hits the water, I will go to a No. 1 spinner and use a No. 0 in the tailouts.

Beyond 62°, many coastal steelhead strains start becoming lethargic. They stop moving and hold in deep holes, taking little interest in anything. Under these conditions, steelhead are also probably experiencing some discomfort and, in some cases, may be in danger of dying if their energy is too heavily taxed. While these steelhead will sometimes strike, I feel that it is unethical to fish for them because an already-suffering fish that is being taxed for every last ounce of energy may not be able to be revived. I like to have the option of being able to successfully release fish that I choose not to keep. As alluded to in an earlier chapter, the State of Indiana Department of Natural Resources (DNR) recommends, for anglers fishing their tiny Lake Michigan tributaries for summer steelhead, not to bother releasing landed fish.

The author poses with his dad on a special occasion: his dad's first summer steelhead! Lori Davis photo

They simply cannot survive the 62° to 65° water once having expended all their energy. In my opinion, it is a very sad state of affairs when our state fisheries people have to advise anglers not to release highly-prized trout in Twentieth Century America. I also question the ethics of anglers, outdoor writers, and any sportsman who would fish these streams and then turn around and claim what great sportsmen they are because they angle for steelhead in "the most sporting way." A *true* sporting way takes into consideration the steelhead's safety and well-being first. I might add that the Indiana DNR never intended the summer steelhead fishery to be a stream fishery. It was designed as an offshore troller's fishery.

Commercially-Made Spinners

Obtaining suitable spinners for summer-run fishing is less of a problem than it is for winter fishing. Brass spinners in sizes 3 and 4 are readily available in French-bladed models.

Bud's, Smolt, Mepps Aglia, Vibrax, etc., will all do a fine job in the low-light conditions outlined above. Even though by my standards these lures tend to be underweighted (with the exception of Smolt) they are more than adequate for typical summer rivers. For the all-important No. 0, No. 1, and No. 2 spinners, I make the following recommendations. First, stick with brass. The best spinners for our purpose will have a brass blade and preferably a brass body. On some models, you will note that the blade is brass but the body is nickel. This is fine. What you don't want is a small spinner with a silver-plated blade. They cost more and will work against your best efforts to hook summer-runs in bright sunlight.

Second, remove all adornments and beads from the blade and body. If you have a spinner with red plastic beads, they can be broken off by squeezing them tightly with pliers. Pressure-sensitive tape should also be removed. This tape is placed on the outside of the blade where it serves no function. It also makes the lure look more gaudy which is undesirable in direct sunlight. If, when removing the tape, a sticky residue remains, this can be easily removed with lacquer thinner. Fluorescent tubing should also be removed. This is easily done with an X-Acto knife or a pair of cosmetic scissors. Once again, the guadiness is not needed. There are exceptions, however. Black tubing, squirrel tails as on Mepps or Woolly Worm tails in the case of the Spinner Bug can be desirable. The key here is that the animal hair be dark — preferably brown or black. Reds and yellows will work against you.

Third, make an effort to purposely tarnish your spinner (sizes 0, 1, and 2 only). This will be a bit more tricky because you don't want to rust the hook. I would protect the hook by wrapping it in Saran wrap and then trying to dull the blade by rolling it in wet dirt and letting it sit outside. Mind you, we are not trying to get the brass to turn black. Rather, we just want to take away all gloss, shine, and sparkle.

As with the larger summer- and winter-run spinners, it is important that the blade spins dependably and on command. However, once you go to a No. 1, or No. 0 blade, it is very difficult if not impossible to achieve the slow-blade spin that is so deadly with winter steelhead. Pulsations on the rod tip become very faint and next to impossible to detect. Don't be concerned about this. As long as that blade is spinning, you are fishing effectively. Once again, it is my feeling that a good French-type blade on a well-balanced spinner is unbeatable. I really wouldn't care what blade you use be it a Swing, Panther Martin type, or Colorado. What I think is important is *dependability*. If when casting the spinner into the water you have to yank on the tip to start the blade, you have got a bad spinner. Why? Many of your summer steelhead will come from the head or shallow riffles . . . right where summer-runs can be found in sunny weather. This means that the instant that spinner hits the water it has got to start working. If you have to yank, you are going to yank it right from an interested steelhead's grasp or the speed of the yank will spook the fish.

One trick anglers use for creating a desired No. 0, No. 1, or No. 2 spinner is to customize an existing model. This is most commonly done with Rooster Tails. As I mentioned in the winter steelhead chapter, these lures spin very undependably relative to the unresponsive swing blades. However, there are a wide variety of colored bodies and matching tails available. This makes it simple to customize. Buy the desired color body. Remove the shaft and discard the blade. Replace with your own French blade on a new shaft using body and hook/tail. (Remember, when held upright, the bottom of the blade should extend slightly beyond the body.) You now have a good spinner.

One more issue deserves mention: the problem of the "Fall Feeders." For reasons that are unknown, late-returning or already-existing summer steelhead will begin to feed in late August and especially in September and October. I read about this phenomenon but never gave it much thought until I received a startling education on the subject when fishing Oregon's summer steelhead. A treble lodged deeply in a steelhead's throat is automatic death. The phenomenon occurs repeatedly in late summer and during the fall. I finally got smart. For the fish's sake, I began switching my trebles to single hooks at about mid-August. I prefer trebles but I also value and respect the steelhead fisheries we are blessed with. As the sign says, "Kill your fish, kill your fishing." For hooks under these circumstances, I recommend a bronze, short-shank, wide-bend hook. The short shank will prevent the fish from taking the lure deeply but the wider bend will allow for greater hooking capacity.

Surface Presentations

Throughout this book, I have stressed the need to fish spinners as close to the bottom as possible. There is one set of circumstances in which a surface presentation is more desirable. This occurs when fishing summer-runs in direct sunlight in water not exceeding six feet and with a temperature of 52° or greater. As I pointed out above, steelhead, under these conditions, will often move into shallow riffly water or right to the edge of a drop-off. I have found that a surface presentation of no more than 12 inches below the surface is very effective in exciting fish into striking. This is, in fact, how steelhead fly fishermen take many of their summer-runs. The key here is to swing the spinner at either the speed of the current or more slowly. Never let a belly get into your line such that the spinner is moving faster than the water. The steelhead won't touch it. This is best avoided by using a long rod of 9 feet or more (I use a 10-foot long ultralight rod) and by keeping all but the terminal one or two feet of line out of the water. In this way, the spinner is most easily controlled.

There are two added tricks to this technique which are not absolutely necessary but which nonetheless increase effectiveness. As the spinner is working its way through a drift, try to make it zigzag in one-half second intervals. This only works if the water is not too fast. Another technique calls for working the spinner a fraction of an inch below the surface such that it creates a wake in the water. This later technique is very difficult to achieve. It will take a lot of practice. Both of these tricks, when employed in the right places under the right conditions will produce thunderous strikes. You haven't seen steelhead strike until they have hit a "zigzagged" or "waked" spinner. You will be shaking and laughing at the same time.

Occasionally, a steelhead will miss on a surface presentation. The worst thing you can do is cast immediately upon retrieval. Rest the water for at least five minutes and then try again. They may hit again.

The Difficult Road to Summer-Run Success

Even though winter steelhead are in greater abundance in more rivers, the truly expert steelheaders catch more summer-runs than they do winter-runs. Why? It has got nothing to do with secret lures or secret rivers. It has more to do with human nature and the freedom of the season. Summer steelhead, in most rivers, have less of a peak season than winter-runs. That is, there are fewer times (if any) during the season when fish are concentrated into a small area where, by sheer numbers, they become easy prey to anglers. The typical fisherman wants to spend time fishing for a particular species only if he thinks he can catch fish easily. The great majority of steelheaders, like all anglers, are fair weather fishermen. If action is not fast and easy, they go for crappie, bass, or trout. (Of course, in winter, they have no choice so they stick with steelhead.) It is typical to see many anglers congregate at a popular summer steelhead site when the word gets out but as soon as angling slows or gets tough, you don't see them until the following year. Most anglers simply do not have the patience, interest, or fanatical love of summer steelhead to keep them in pursuit of these fish. What this does is leave miles upon miles of river open for large portions of the season to people like me (and maybe you?) who would never consider fishing for anything but summer-runs during the summer and fall months.

The author releases a Siletz River steelhead. Asa Pearl photo

And, because the rivers are always in good shape during the summer, there are far more fishable days in the summer than there are during the winter. I fish drifts on the McKenzie where I guarantee you that I am the only serious steelheader who comes through after mid-September. Sure, the fish are spread out and their numbers are modest but, if I am the only one fishing, what do you think happens? What's interesting here is that I don't do well during the peak, that time when boat traffic is bumper-to-bumper. I wait for this carnival to pass. They never stay long. Then I get down to business. The peak of the McKenzie run arrives in late June. My best days come in August, September, and October.

Is this all there is to it? No, that's only a small part . . . the beginning or perhaps the appetizer. The greatest factor in your success will be your own persistence, a burning desire to explore, discover, and experiment without becoming discouraged. And it is difficult. Do you know that when my wife and I moved to Oregon, I had never caught a summer-run? I fished for days on end before I ever touched one. I would get angry, be terribly frustrated. My wife would say over and over, "Why don't you take it easy. Don't go back for a few days." My arms were sore because I wasn't used to drift-boating and my hands would be swollen, but I would always reply, "I'm going back tomorrow." Very slowly, I started to move forward. For a time, I averaged a fish every fifth trip, then it got down to every second trip. Today, it is rare that I come away from the McKenzie without having landed one, two, or three steelhead. And the four- and five-fish days are not uncommon. Okay. Now you might ask, "I've got the persistence, where do I start?"

I suggest selecting one or two spinner drifts, drifts with shallow, well-defined water, and then sticking to them come hell or high water. If a summer stream has a stable, consistent run in the summer (even in modest numbers), you can assume that steelhead will be distributed in all parts of the river once the run has gotten under way. I would pick a drift in the lower part of the river. This way, you know fish are coming through if they are catching them in the upper drifts. Try to stay away from popular drifts. The "I'm

Hatchery steelhead, 9½ and 13½ pounds, taken on successive casts from the McKenzie. Lori Davis photo

gonna beat you to the next hole" game will interrupt your concentration and inhibit your thought processes. Learn these one or two drifts like you've never learned a drift before. Cover everything, try everything, and, most impor-

tantly, study everything. You will be amazed at what will happen over time. You will discover where the steelhead hold and how best to approach them. You may go through ten or twenty times and think you know the drift but you will keep learning more and more subtle things that will make a difference on future trips. Patterns will emerge in all aspects of angling — holding water identification, approach, spinner selection. Becoming an expert on "your" drift will greatly aid you in quickly mastering new drifts. But I want to stress that mastery comes via careful, intensive study of a little rather than jumping all over the river from day to day in search of magic. This reminds me of a fellow here in Eugene who is a follow-the-sheep steelheader. If someone tells him that they had a good day on the Dot's[1] to Hendrick's Bridge McKenzie River drift, that's where you will find him the following day. On the day after, you might see him twenty miles upstream at Finn Rock. *He knows the river but he doesn't know how to fish it.* He has never given himself a chance to learn anything. To do consistently well with summer-runs, this is a necessary condition.

There's another point I wish to make. I, like everyone else, read the hunting and fishing reports that appear each Thursday in local papers. Whether living in Eugene, Ann Arbor, Cleveland, or Madison, Wisconsin, I have found these reports to, in most cases, be a very poor indicator of what is happening on the stream. Most local outdoor columnists are a jack-of-all-trades. Sure, they're interested in steelhead but they also take an interest in lingcod and crappie. The reports they get are generally outdated by the time you read them and, if not the latter, then they are often unreliable. If the columnist is an avid steelheader himself, chances are he will protect "his" stream or his friends' streams from the masses.

The 1983 summer steelhead season was a good example of what I mean. Only twice during the summer did the fishing report in our local newspaper allude to the McKenzie summer-runs and this was early in the season. From July 15th on, there were few times that I came away from the McKenzie without having landed less than two steelhead. Supposedly, the fishing was so poor that it wasn't even worth it for the fishing report to say: "Steelhead fishing — poor." The moral is this: If you want to find out how the fishing is on a particular stream and you don't have a reliable source, then get into the car, drive there, and fish it.

Having read "The Key to Summer-Run Success" to this point, you may be disappointed. I haven't talked about any easy tricks. Quite frankly, there are none. But I want to demonstrate that *attitude* is such a large part of the game. Talk to any number of summer steelhead experts and ask about their initial experiences. More than likely, they were terribly frustrated when they began to fish summer-runs but they refused to quit or take comfort in other anglers' expectations. In the final analysis, I truly believe that the road to consistent summer-run fishing is a positive state of mind — one which perseveres and is open to new techniques and approaches and one which develops an *ultra-sensitivity* to the river environment. Beyond this, I am at a loss to offer anything more.

[1]Dot's Restaurant was changed to Elaine's Restaurant around 1981 but burned down in 1983. However, the boat launch is still there.

Chapter 9

Rods, Reels, and Lines

EVERY TIME I SEE THE ABOVE TITLE IN A fishing book, I cringe. Typically, the author tells the reader "to do this," "use that," "never use those," or "do it like this." What you end up with is a chapter that describes the author's personal outfit as the ultimate or only outfit. If there were only one outfit you could use to successfully catch steelhead, everyone would be using it. The fact is, a hundred experts use a hundred different outfits. I work on the premise that no one outfit is best at all times, for all anglers, and in all conditions. There are no absolutes, only variations. The goal of this chapter is to describe the benefits and disadvantages of different types of rods, reels, and lines. More often than not, the choice of one thing over another is a trade-off of one quality for another.

Rods

All rod tapers are built on a continuum that exists between two extremes. On one extreme, fast-action rods bend only in the upper one-quarter of the rod. The rest of the rod is stiff. On the other extreme, slow-action rods, the entire rod bends into one continuous loop over the entire length. There are many in-between variations. The advantage of fast-action rods is that a hook can be set very hard and very quickly. The stiff backbone in the rod allows one to "put the screws" to a fish that needs to be turned. The disadvantages are casting is done in a quick motion and it is difficult to be accurate. Casting distance is limited. The wrist does the work in casting. This leads to greater fatigue. Fish can easily break lines or pull hooks free because there is relatively little shock-absorbing of the line by the rod. Such rods tend to be heavy. Slow-action rods are slow hook setters because more of the rod has to bend before direct line tension is realized. They lack backbone which means that it is difficult to horse fish when needed. When casting, the rod

does the work. Casting distance and accuracy are maximized. Fish have a difficult time breaking or tearing loose the hook because the rod gives every time the fish pulls. *Observation:* 1) Distance and accuracy are critical to success; 2) steelheaders greatly exaggerate the amount of power needed to set a hook with large winter-run spinners; 3) no back bone is bad, too much backbone is worse.

Steelhead rods come in various lengths. The typical length used is 8½ to 9 feet. A short rod of 8½ to 9 feet does not cast as far and the shorter length means less line control. These shorter rods are comfortable to handle and will give less fatigue. A long steelhead rod, 9½ to 10½ feet, casts farther. The added length allows the angler to pick line off the water, thereby allowing one to work the spinner more deeply and generally more accurately. A longer length, in general, causes greater fatigue. *Observation:* Length is more critical for summer-runs because small, light spinners must be cast long distances. Length also helps pick line off the water thereby allowing one to work spinners deeper. If fatigue is not a concern, it would seem that the longer rod would add some advantage. The fatigue factor is reduced by using fly blanks for spinning rods.

Contrary to some manufacturers' claims, graphite *is* more sensitive than boron. Boron has a quicker recovery rate which means greater hook-setting. Both are more sensitive and lighter than glass although graphite is lighter than boron. Glass is far cheaper than both graphite and boron. *Observation:* All three materials work well. Boron, in most cases, is a poor value. Stay away from glass if fatigue is a problem. Pulsations on the rod tip are important for winter-runs. A more sensitive rod aids in the feel of pulsations.

Reels

You basically have two choices: Open-face bail and level-wind. Level-winds have superior drag systems, in part because of their design. They can be cast a long distance but suffer from backlash. Perfect balance is impossible to design into a level-wind and the hand must exert effort at all times to keep the reel stable. The result is greater fatigue. Level-winds are awkward to cast in many positions — for example, back-handed casts at 10:00. Level-winds are excellent tools to "tail" with. That is, a spinner can be worked

A rare shot of Asa Pearl, pictured here with two steelies. Pearl is an excellent steelhead spinner fisherman and has been a true innovator of technique. Jed Davis photo

downstream with great ease after it has swung around. Open-face drags are temperamental because drag is created from a 90-degree angle. They can be cast a maximum distance only if the rod is designed to match the reel. (It is critical as to where line is choked off as coils enter the stripper guide. The stripper guide must be the right size and placed in the right spot. They are typically too small on mass-produced rods.) Open-face reels balance themselves under the rod. There is no need to hold it in place as with level-wind. The result is less fatigue. Open-face reels are much easier to cast from all positions than level-winds. Open-face reels tail awkwardly. *Observation:* Unless you are a real pro with a level-wind, I would stick to open-face. Automatic bail open-face reels are poorly suited to steelhead spinner fishing.

Lines

A spinner is a very active lure, so much so that when it swings by a fish, it catches the fish's attention to the exclu-

sion of the monofilament. Furthermore, spinners are not posing as natural drifters. Thus, they do not have to necessarily appear as if they are flowing at the same speed as the current. What this all means is that whether you use 6-, 8-, 10-, or 12-pound test, all other factors being equal, a lighter line will in most cases not result in a significantly better catch. However, heavier line will have two disadvantages. First, its thicker diameter will result in greater water resistance which means that in water that is fast and deep, you will have more difficulty in working the spinner deeply. Second, heavier lines come off the spool less smoothly. This means that as one goes up in line strength, casting distance and accuracy are sacrificed. *Observation:* Most anglers stay within the 8- to 12-pound range. If you are fishing a trophy area such as Washington State's East Fork Lewis with its occasional 20- to 30-pound steelhead, you may want to go to a higher pound test line.

When choosing to fish a particular strength mono with a given spinner, one should consider whether the line is strong enough to drive home the hook. This is especially true with the lowest test monos. The larger the hook, the broader the point and the more difficult it is to drive home a hook. When using No. 2 round-bend trebles (used on No. 5 spinners), it is not wise to go below 8-pound. On a No. 4 treble (used on No. 3 and No. 4 spinners), 6-pound would seem to be the limit. Because spinner fishing takes such a toll on lines via abrasion and twist, one is really taking a chance by fishing with a strength below 4-pound regardless of the size spinner fished.

Closing Words on Steelhead

In *Steelhead Drift Fishing,* author Bill Luch made several references to the difficulty of describing on paper what really happens when fishing for steelhead. His message seemed to imply that while books are helpful, they often fall short of giving you what you need to know in order to be consistently successful. I agree but would put it a little bit differently. Book knowledge is only as good as the stream experience you have to match it with. The total amount of time spent with steelhead, be it through home study or river experience, must be heavily weighted for the latter. I would certainly be flattered if someone told me that they read this book four times or intensely studied various chapters but in no way can this writing serve as a substitute or as compensation. You have got to put in the time and not only when the fishing is hot. It is just as important, if not more so, to put in the time when fishing is difficult or conditions are less than optimal. It will force you to become a better steelheader. My personal discovery of how to take McKenzie summer-runs in bright sunshine in the middle of a hot day was accomplished not only against the "better" advice of local McKenzie River experts but also at a time of day when the hot summer sun beating down on the open water can make for a grueling experience that leaves one physically drained. I always used to think that time spent on the river was only valuable if I caught a steelhead. I now know that those times where I skunked were just as important because in looking back on each of those experiences, I learned a lot about what not to do and when not to be on the river. In other words, you have to lose in order to learn how to win.

Chapter 10

The Most Frequently Asked Steelhead-Spinner Questions

HERE ARE ANSWERS TO THE MOST FREQUENTLY asked steelhead spinner questions. The questions cover topics discussed in previous chapters of this book, plus a few additional areas of interst.

Q. What is your favorite spinner?

A. I don't have one. Give me a set of environmental conditions and I will tell you what spinner is likely to produce the best results in those conditions. Most anglers are oriented toward a "secret" or "magical" lure that is to be used for everything. From my standpoint, the *real secret* is learning how to use environmental conditions such as lighting, water temperature, and water clarity to make a choice of spinners.

Q. I read a number of articles in Great Lakes' magazines where the authors state that 80 percent or better of all Great Lakes steelhead are taken on spawn (roe, eggs). Doesn't this prove that spawn is superior to all other baits, including spinners?

A. No, it only means that more fish are caught on spawn because more people fish it. The same could be said for hot-shotting in the Pacific Northwest. Show me ten anglers who catch between a hundred and two-hundred steelhead per year using spawn; I'll show you ten of the same who use spinners exclusively. People get hooked on bait as children. Using worms for bluegills can be very convincing. Most people never get over those first convincing worm and bobber experiences. Yet, the world's top bass pros rarely use live bait. Now you explain that one to me.

Q. I've been fishing steelhead for ten years with a partner who is strictly a bait fisherman. I use lures — spinners and spoons. We take twenty trips per year and I outfish him once every two years and yet you claim to do as well as anglers using other methods?

A. Get a new partner. Your ten-year partner is probably seeing the river as a drifter would and should. More than likely he is taking you to good Corky and Egg water which is not necessarily best suited to your lures. He is also probably passing up water which he cannot fish but which otherwise would be great for you. Your only other option is to sue him for ten years of mental anguish.

Q. The only way I can catch a summer-run is to be on the river at dawn and hope to hook a steelhead before the sun hits the water. Why is this?

A. You didn't mention what you were using but I bet its's a big Stee-lee or large, flashy spinner. These lures are fine in low-light, summer conditions but, when the sun hits the water, forget it! These lures spook summer steelhead. You have to go down to small No. 1 and No. 2 spinners that are dull and dark, and start fishing the shallow riffles and drop-offs.

Q. I fish the Maple Island area of Michigan's Muskegon River. I know exactly where the fish hold. Inspired by a spinner article, I fish spinners and get nothing. Then I switch to drift-fishing and get action immediately. What do you say to that?

A. I fish some long, wide flats on Oregon's McKenzie River. I know exactly where the fish hold. Inspired by drift fishermen, I fish drift gear and get nothing; then I switch to spinners and get action immediately. What do you say to that?

Moral 1: No one method is the best in all rivers, under all conditions, at all times of the day.

Moral 2: You can be fishing the proper bait. It does not mean you are fishing it effectively.

In regard to Moral 2, this is the biggest mistake anglers make with regard to spinners. They think that there is nothing to it so they don't bother to develop technique. This ultimately results in poor catches and they lose interest. Like steelhead fly-fishing, steelhead spinner fishing requires much more skill than drift-fishing or hot-shotting to make consistently good catches. In other words, you have to reach a certain threshold of skill before you start doing well. However, once you reach this threshold level of skill, the effectiveness of the technique will humble you.

Q. I do a combination of spinner fishing and hot-shotting for winter steelhead. The best spinner for this fishing is silver-plated and, yet, I have my best luck with a green or dark red Wee-Wart when hot-shotting. Why are two different colors so effective at the same time, and on two different types of lures?

A. Spinners are *attractors* — nothing more. Wobblers like the Wee-Wart pose as live baitfish. An attractor is trying to excite fish into hitting by being as gaudy as possible — hence, silver. A wobbler should appear as natural as possible. For winter-runs, the conditions are generally gray or dark with off-colored water. Thus, an attractor should be as bright and eye-catching as possible. A baitfish can only reflect as much light as is available. Thus, when it's dark, the wobbler should be dark. When it's light, the wobbler should be light. In the typical conditions we fish in winter, dark green or dark red would be good choices.

A Summer Green spinner fooled this summer-run. Craig Rosner photo

Q. If you didn't silver plate your winter steelhead spinners, how well eo you think you would do?

A. As I always say, skill is the most important factor. But, I would also say that under typical, off-colored conditions of winter, the silver is about 20 percent more effective. In small and/or clear streams, I doubt that it would matter unless the water was exceptionally cold under which conditions silver would be useful as a maximum exciter; or in very dark lighting, and/or roily water, under which conditions, silver would have more visibility.

Q. Why are reddish adornments good in winter and green adornments good in summer?

A. I always fear this question because, at best, I can only give an educated guess. Red maintains its true color at great depths or in poor visibility or in low light. This aids in attraction because the lure is more visible during times when you need it most. In summer, water is generally clear and greens blend in well with underwater flora such as algae. Thus, green lends presence but does not provide such a contrast so as to startle steelhead.

Q. I've gotten discouraged trying to fish spinners for winter-runs because I never feel as if I am on the bottom. I've been using a No. 4 Bud's.

A. A decent spinner but very underweighted. I suggest making half-ounce No. 5s or using a Quality Tackle Smolt. You might also try lead-bodied worm weights for bodies. If this doesn't do it, you are fishing in the wrong places. Very deep and fast West Coast slot water is good for drift-fishing. Look for shallow or well-defined rivers.

Q. I think your last article was baloney. I do very well with Panther Martins and you think they are interfior to Mepps type blades. I'll match you fish for fish!

A. You should fish what you have confidence in. My only complaint with Panther Martin is that the slow-blade spin that is so utterly deadly on steelhead is harder to achieve with a Panther Martin blade. But, it does sound like you have a lot of skill. Skill comes first.

Q. I, like you, have had great luck with spinners on steelhead. What is the history of steelhead spinner fishing? Are there any organizations or clubs?

A. To the best of my knowledge (and I'm always on the lookout), I know of no organizations, clubs, or networks. Mepps has a spinner club but its only purpose seems to be the increased promotion and sale of their products. There are a number of people in the Great Lakes states and in the Pacific Northwest who have dedicated a tremendous amount of time to the method. I suppose that I am one of these anglers. We all do well, although we all do it a little bit differently. I think that, for many of these individuals, the acquisition of knowledge and skill is a personal thing which they do not feel compelled to share. They compete only with themselves and want to be left alone. I know two individuals who are convinced that going after steelhead on spinners is the ultimate method and don't want to share information for fear that it might eventually lead to stream competition. Several other anglers have voiced disappointment over the fact that spinner fishing has gotten relatively little publicity from the greater steelhead fraternity. It is their own fault. They want people to be interested but choose to keep much of their technique a secret. They aren't very prolific either. Steelhead spinner history? I know of none. Mepps, the first French-bladed spinner, has been in the U. S. for 27 years. I found that out on a shortwave radio broadcast. Twenty-seven years is not much time. Perhaps our Zane Greys, Haig-Browns, and Al Knudsons have just been born.

Q. Do you fish steelhead with spinners exclusively?

A. For winter steelhead, no. I like to fish a variety of rivers but some are simply not well-suited for spinner fishing. Ninety-percent of my winter-runs come on spinners, five percent on eggs, and another five percent on plugs. In summer, nearly all fish come on spinners. A few come on flies. I identify myself as a steelhead spinner angler but I am also a student of steelhead fishing. I'm always fooling with egg recipes. I like to keep up with things.

Q. Do you find that knowledge of other steelhead methods helps you in acquiring skill?

A. Yes and no. Steelhead spinner fishing requires unique skills that cannot be gained overnight or as a result of having fished other methods (and that includes Steelees). Still, any kind of steelhead or general fishing knowledge will be of value.

Q. I like fishing spinners but dislike using large No. 4

and No. 5 spinners. What's the prospect of taking winter-runs on small spinners?

A. Not bad . . . if you find the right stream. I have experimented with silver-plated No. 2s on small streams that are barely large enough for drift boats. At times, I have done well. What you have to do is work each area longer and harder because the smaller spinner will excite from a smaller radius.

Q. Which is more difficult to take on spinners, winter-runs or summer-runs?

A. A really tough question. They tax different areas of skill. In winter, you have to know how to manipulate the spinner close to the bottom and with a slow spin. In summer, you have to know where to look for the fish and you have to know which spinner will work given varied and changing environmental conditions. Both are easy to take if you reach a certain level of understanding and skill. It takes patience and dedication to get to that point.

Q. A lot of people say drift-fishing eggs and bobbers is the most productive steelhead method. How do you respond to those comments?

A. I get these comments all the time. First, I don't fish spinners for steelhead because I think it is the best method. I fish spinners because I *like the act* of fishing spinners over and above everything else. I'm attracted to the pursuit and challenge. It also has a certain finesse not possible with other monofilament methods. Second, and maybe this is what you wanted a response to, is that on a daily or yearly basis, I do as well as any steelheader. I rarely skunk and a majority of my days are multiple-fish days. The point is this: If they do better with eggs, so be it. I don't really care. I'm content. But, you'll never hear me say, "I never get enough."

Q. Is there anything to watch for in terms of how steelhead strike?

A. At times, but not often, the steelhead will take the spinner like a bobber and eggs. With winter-runs, I find this usually occurs in deep, slow runs with water temperatures below 39°. Summer-runs do it also but not in a predictable manner. The moral is that anytime you feel the lure stop, set the hook.

Q. I live in Portland. As you know, there are so many rivers to choose from. Could you recommend a spinner river?

A. I know of your rivers but haven't fished them. But this is the ideal I would search for: A shallow stream/drift with many obstacles, pools, pockets, riffles, gravel bars, obstructions. If you can look at the water's surface and know what is under the water, this is the ideal. Stay away from deep slots with fast water. It's difficult and not fun to fish such areas.

Q. You say you've fished all steelhead methods. What attracts you to spinners?

A. Two parts to this answer: First, it's the closest thing to fly-fishing. I love to cast spinners and enjoy placing a spinner "on a dime." Lots of finesse and grace. In fact, I use a fly rod and a spinning reel that functions as a fly reel. Second, I can cover a tremendous amount of water one-hundred percent effectively in a very short time. I don't have to worry about snags or whether the water is too fast or too slow. Not true with other methods.

Q. Are there any environmental conditions under which you won't angle for steelhead?

A. Muddy water, heavy rain aside, yes. For winter steelhead, cold east wind in low water. For summer-runs, uncharacteristically cold night with cool winds on the following day of ten miles per hour or more.

Q. How do you compare Great Lakes versus Northwest steelheading in terms of spinner technique?

A. Spinner fishing for steelhead is easier in the Great Lakes. The rivers tend to be smaller, much more gentle, shallower. Because there is relatively less good holding water in Great Lakes tributaries, fish tend to be more concentrated. But, then, we have Northwest rivers that remind me of Michigan, and a few Michigan rivers that are distinctly Northwest in nature.

Q. A lot of people use lead worm weights in spinners. I get the impression that you are not very fond of them.

A. You are right. They are not fun to fish although effective. They are heavy, bulky, and make big splashes. I feel as if I'm trying to cast an anchor. I also don't like the idea of a prized steelhead trying to fight with an ounce of lead in its mouth. To me, this is like trolling for rainbow trout with those large Cousin Carl and Ford Fender flashers. That junk is so heavy and bulky that all sport is taken away. Why not just go to the fish market and buy trout already dressed? It would end up being cheaper, and you would save time, thereby giving yourself time to *fish*. I stay away from water that would require me to fish spinners with worm weights.

Anglers fish the east side of the 6th Street Dam on the Grand River in downtown Grand Rapids. It is remarkable that such an excellent fishery exists in the heart of a downtown metropolitan area. Jed Davis photo

Q. Do you follow any rules in terms of using different color adornments on your spinners?

A. Reds, oranges, and pinks from mid-November on or when water is 49° or below. Greens when water is above 50° and the river has "blossomed." That is, the river becomes alive with its typical summer "life." Black is generally reliable for all temperatures.

Q. Will crowding or heavy river traffic affect the steelhead's disposition to hit a spinner?

A. Yes, I think so. It is my personal belief that steelhead have to be aggressive and secure to strike large spinners. If I'm fishing a small stream with heavy boat traffic, I go to drift gear. On a large stream, it doesn't matter that much. There are times where I have been behind three or four boats on the Siuslaw and did very well.

Q. Are there any books available that would be good reading for the study of steelhead spinner fishing?

A. Yes, but they are not on spinner fishing. I regard fly fishing and spinner fishing as being very closely related. In fact, I often think of myself as fishing "metal flies." Except for dry-fly techniques, the approaches are nearly identical. There is a tremendous volume of fly fishing literature. Anything on steelhead or Atlantic salmon will provide valuable perspectives. Three books come immediately to mind: *The Atlantic Salmon* by Lee Wulff, *Steelhead Fly Fishing and Flies* by Trey Combs, and *Greased Line Fishing for Salmon [and Steelhead]* by Jock Scott. I also spend a considerable amount of time studying fly patterns for Atlantic salmon and steelhead. I will study groups of related patterns and look for themes and color relationships that might prove productive for steelhead spinners. Then I try to convert the concept into a spinner.

Q. How many spinners do you go through a year?

A. For winter-runs, I always carry 12 spinners with me.

I've lost as many as ten No. 5s an outing, but average between two and four lost per outing. Over a season, I go through between 140 and 200. That's why I make my own. I probably spend more days fishing for summer-runs but lose maybe twenty spinners per season. The smaller the spinner, the less you lose. If you lost a lot of No. 1s and No. 2s, you're doing something very unusual, like casting onto a lot of branches.

Q. Does technique or spinner choice change from river to river?

A. Amazing consistency both intra-regional and inter-regional. Spinners are attractors — nothing more. You are not imitating a fly hatch or a specific baitfish. Since most all steelhead have the same basic nature, they will react similarly to the same colors, finishes, or sizes given similar specific environmental conditions. There are, however, special circumstances. For example, one of my Oregon winter rivers seems to produce with silver and black instead of the usual silver and fire orange. These cases are the exception rather than the rule.

Q. What initially inspired you to try black blades?

A. I wanted to present the darkest, most nonthreatening spinner to summer-runs in such a way that they would take notice without being spooked.

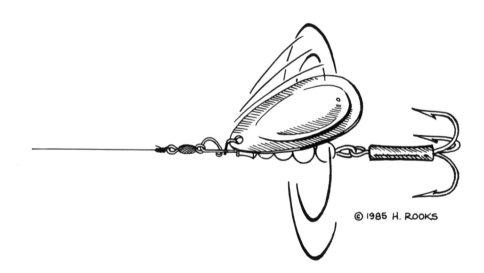

© 1985 H. ROOKS

Chapter 11

Encounters with Steelhead

THIS IS A COLLECTION OF STORIES . . . memorable moments that have taken place during the course of my steelheading career. All of these stories have one thing in common; that is, all the fish were taken with spinners.

There are literally hundreds of stories that could have been told. I had to choose. This was difficult because how can one exciting moment be more exciting or better than the next? All are precious but this book can only be so large. I chose a variety of experiences which touched upon different aspects of angling: the unexpected, the humorous, the unusual, the philosophical, and of course, the triumphs. Some anglers define a good fishing experience in terms of quantity or poundage — hardly the case here. None of the battles recounted involved trophy-sized fish or record quantities. For me, a truly great encounter with a steelhead is one that speaks as a metaphor for man's relation to his fish or to the environment. Perhaps a particular battle was not so unusual but, just the same, a personal mood, the ambience or the moment may have caused me to experience new feelings or achieve new levels of understanding. With that introduction, here are some of my greatest moments.

Double Take

I was having a good day of fishing on one of my favorite drifts. Because the water was higher than usual, a perfect pool was created just above a descending chute of white water. On my first cast, I momentarily hooked a steelhead but lost it. I continued casting, still lamenting over the fish I had just hooked and lost. I finally turned to cast in another direction; this produced a solid strike. The fish jumped and then took off between two protruding willows and raced downstream. Within a few seconds, this steelhead peeled off all of my line plus most of the fluorescent backing I use

as a warning that I only have a few yards of line left. I immediately pulled up the anchor and began chasing the fish but the line got caught onto one of the willows. I had no choice but to break the line. Within four casts, I had lost two nice steelhead.

Somewhat discouraged, I tied a new spinner onto the little line I had left and began to cast into the next pool. As I began retrieving the spinner out of the water, I noticed a loop of line that had caught on the tines of the treble. I knew it was the line I had lost and was anxious to retrieve it. To add insult to injury, the loop fell off the spinner before I was able to grab it. A few more casts did not produce a steelhead or the lost line. I moved down to the next pool and hooked my lost line again. Instead of trying to retrieve it, I pulled up the anchor and let the boat float down to where I had hooked it.

As I finally grabbed the line, a fish splashed ten feet to my left. Anxious to tie a blood knot, I had to figure out which end of the loop was free and which end had the fish. The last thing I wanted to do was end up fighting a steelhead with a bare line in hand. I gently pulled on each end of the loop and after a few seconds was able to determine which end of the loop had the fish. I gathered in the other end, ripped off my lure and tied a blood knot, all the time hoping the steelhead would not move. Now ready to fight the fish, I discovered that the darn steelhead had wrapped the line around a number of obstructions. So I spent the next several minutes rowing all over the pool and somehow I was able to free all the line. I dropped the anchor, got the net ready, and the fight was on. Being rested, the steelhead got a chance to do it all over again. A few minutes later and securely in the net, I roared! A one-in-a-thousand shot had come home.

The Unstoppables

The Unstoppables, as I call them, are wild winter steelhead that return to their natal streams in March and April. One might argue that these Oregon steelhead are true spring fish. Whatever you might call them, it is the fighting ability and physical characteristics that drew my attention to these unique steelhead. The two or three small streams in which I have found them get so little pressure throughout the year that I have found only one other person who has shared similar experiences. On the other hand, I am reluctant to say anything to fellow anglers for fear of finding other boats on the same drifts. But let me say that these are not quantity fisheries. Anyone approaching these streams in the hope of "limiting out" really belongs on a more popular stream. While I generally pick up one or two spawned-out hatchery fish on each drift, there is maybe only a 40 percent chance of tying tips with one of these hair-trigger torpedoes. Simply, I am led to beleive that few of these unique steelhead exist. But when I think back to some of the encounters I have had with these fish, the extra travel and expense seem to be but a minor sacrifice.

Wildcat bridge crosses Wildcat Creek just as it dumps into the Siuslaw. This has been the site of many a steelhead battle for many generations of steelheaders. Jed Davis photo

The name "unstoppable" of course comes from the fight. The typical steelhead, upon being hooked, often twists and wiggles, then makes a run ending in a roll or jump. From the moment an unstoppable hits, it immediately becomes apparent that a connection has been made with something a bit different. These fish simply do not stop moving for the first 45 seconds as they run in an unpredictable pattern. While they jump in all the traditional ways, their distinguishing characteristic seems to be a porpoise-like movement out of the water. Sometimes they porpoise two or three times in succession.

You might automatically think these steelhead to be large. This is not the case. The largest may have gone ten pounds but the most memorable encounters seem to come from six- or seven-pound fish. But more than anything else, one is totally at the mercy of these steelhead in the initial moments of battle.

Of the steelhead I have landed, each displayed a distinctive beauty that livens the senses and humbles the soul. The body is sleek, perfectly proportioned and radiates an ambience of speed and strength. The fins are generally without flaw as these fish have traveled only a few miles from the Pacific Ocean. The tail seems oversized, looking similar to the tail of an Atlantic salmon. In many ways, these steelhead

remind me of various color photographs I have seen of Alaskan and British Columbian steelhead. The bright fish are more of a matted silver. Those with colored gillplates and flank display a subtle pastel rose hue. After capturing and releasing one, there really is not too much to say. Words would spoil the moment.

The unstoppables have shown me what can result when fish are managed for the fish's sake rather than for the sportsmen's sake. Fisheries management geared towards the propagation of native or wild stocks results in a consistently higher quality steelhead. Survival rates are also enhanced because naturally-produced fish are more intact with their environment.

While in Michigan I used to fish for steelhead on redds but after seeing what can result from the propogation of native and wild stocks, I wouldn't do this type of fishing anymore. Hatchery steelhead offer great sport but there is something special about fishing for wild steelhead. It is not something that is measured in terms of weight, size or quantity. It is simply a feeling . . . a good feeling that goes right to your head and right to your heart. So, it is no wonder that when late February or March rolls around that my orientation changes a bit. It is not the big fish, the many fish, or the steelhead steaks that I am interested in. Rather, it is to be in touch with something very special, to feel its awesomeness, and to somehow be part of its world by entering into a struggle, if only for a few seconds, with these incredible late-returning steelhead: The Unstoppables.

Steel Fish and a Tin Man

It was late January and the water on the Umpqua was at a low winter level. While others waited for a freshet, I was eager to be on the river. Spinner fishing for steelhead is ideal in these conditions. About one-third of the way through my drift, I approached a small run that under normal conditions would never hold fish. But for now, at least, it looked promising.

I cast my No. 5 silver spinner into the short slot that lay in front of me. Being fast and deep, it was not the type of place where one could easily drift a spinner along the bottom. The slot was perhaps six feet deep. On my first cast, the spinner traveled quickly at about three feet under the surface.

At almost the instant the spinner began to work, a large silver flash made a swirl and was immediately gone. My first thought was that the fish struck but missed because I felt a jolt but then . . . nothing. My sudden dejection was negated a few seconds later. As I unenthusiastically reeled up slack, I suddenly felt resistance. The fight was on. This fish, in a matter of one or two seconds, had apparently struck very hard, very quickly and then immediately swam down to the river's bottom, then upstream without realizing he had been hooked.

I was matched with a ten-pound buck, caught close to tidewater and in the very peak of condition. What made this such an unforgettable fight was that we had to fight it out in close quarters. There was simply no place else the fish wanted to go and there was nowhere I could take him. This was also a fish that did not rest or sulk. He would expend every last ounce of energy until exhausted or defeated. The jumps, the streaks, the head-shaking and twisting were all done from close range. Power versus power, determination versus determination, will versus will. The struggle felt close and very direct. I eventually won the battle but that is not what seemed to be important. There was something more.

I pulled my boat over to the shore. I took this perfect specimen of a steelhead and laid it on a large rock in such a way that its awesome beauty would be visually maximized. I had many different thoughts. Why did I kill this fish without thinking it over? Was I a hero? Did the challenge justify the keep? I delved further. I had been as close to a steelhead's fight for freedom as I possibly could have been. I recounted the fish's life endeavor: mergansers, sharks, seals, other fishes, parasites, pollution. And, even having made it this far, there was still more to encounter: anglers, finding a mate, the rigors of spawning, surviving extreme exhaustion, avoiding opportunistic saltwater creatures. There was no rest. The burden was always just beginning. Did this not mean anything or was I too saturated in my own self?

I now felt a bit stupid and very mortal. Looking passionately at the solid steel mask that graced the steelhead's head and crown, the word then hit me — "crown." Here was the real hero — good to meet but maybe best left alone.

Strange Friends

I was fishing the McKenzie in early August. I approached a popular tailout, anchoring my boat in a position such that I could spot steelhead lying on the break. Steelhead holding in this particular spot generally do not hit due to their vulnerability and angle to the sun at the time when I typically make my approach.

Quietly standing up, I saw two large fish holding side by side in the fast current. At first, I assumed that they were large steelhead for it was a month too early for the spring chinook to be spawning. Then I changed my mind — two chinook. Puzzled, I finally realized that the larger fish was a male springer and the smaller of the two was a large summer steelhead. Both held steady over a redd, side by side. They became increasingly nervous and restless due to my presence. The chinook was first to move. He would six inches upstream and the steelhead would follow, always trying to maintain a perfect parallel alignment with the chinook. They moved upstream and eventually out of sight as the water they travelled in got progressively deeper.

I returned the following day. I anchored in the exact same spot. As I slowly stood up, I saw the steelhead. It was the same one, no question about it but the chinook was gone. This summer-run was no longer holding on the redd. A summer-spawning summer-run would have been highly unusual but had it been one I would have left it alone. Convinced that it was just another steelhead, I cast a black-bladed No. 1 spinner to it. In this situation, on a tailout and in direct sunlight, my experience has shown that they will spook via the presentation of anything brighter or larger. The fish ignored my offering and, in anger, moved to a new position directly below the boat. All I had to do was dangle it in front of his nose. He would not touch it. I could not go any duller or darker so I went larger. He ignored a No. 2 but did not spook. Interesting. I went to a No. 3 brass with kelly green adornments. I was sure he'd spook. I swung the spinner directly below him until it was two inches above his nose and I kept it there. He moved from side to side a few times, then slowly rose and inhaled it.

The fight was unimportant. What was more significant is the fact that this steelhead's behavior was the negation of everything I have learned about summer steelhead.

The Umpqua Never Fails

It was late October and several rainy periods during the prior weeks had pushed river levels to beyond their summer norm. After a few successful fall salmon trips, I longed for my summer steelhead streams. I wasn't yet ready to say goodbye. Maybe I needed one more experience to tell me that it was over for the year.

I do very little shore fishing for steelhead in Oregon. Most all of my fishing is done from a boat but I do have one spot on the North Umpqua that I like to occasionally walk from when in the mood.

The morning light showed the river to be higher than I had ever seen it in the summer or fall months. Naturally, it was deserted, as sportsmen were either hunting or looking forward to winter steelhead. I worked the entire area very carefully but could only manage one small coho that was released.

Approaching the very end of the public access, I asked myself how long it had been since I had gotten skunked here. I waded into the river as deeply as I could go in order to reach what looked to be a perfect summer-run pocket that had been created by the high water. One accurate toss of my spinner and this would be the last cast of the day.

With all of my weight behind it, I finally was able to reach my target! The spinner quickly traveled downstream with a steelhead in hot pursuit. As it swung around in very, very fast water, the fish grabbed it. His instinct was to move up into the pool but the resistance of the water was so great that he was forced to go downstream. Once a good summer-run decides to head downstream, it's trouble, especially if you are fishing from shore with limited access.

In this case, 50 yards of white water lay beneath that tailout. What's more, the riverbed descended into a gorge from which I would eventually be fighting the fish from 40 feet above the river. I saw it all coming. No sooner did he head downstream than I knew it was hopeless to try and stop him. What was I to do, break the line? No, even if it was a fish I was to lose, the feel of that throbbing sea-run rainbow at the end of my line was something I wanted to preserve for as long as possible.

I followed the steelhead, stumbling over rocks in a chase that followed the gorge for a long way downstream. Slowing him was an act in futility for every time I pulled, he pulled harder . . . and won.

At the end of the white water section, a small slack pool lay to the right. There was a tailout that led into a five-foot drop and some more white water. More importantly though was the fact that this was the end for me. The cliff from which I was standing suddenly ended. I could walk no further from where I stood. There was a path leading down to the water's edge but there was simply no way I could hold the rod in hand because the path meandered its way through some large firs. Considering the scenario, my strategy was set into motion.

Even though the steelhead had dictated the rules up until this time, he did show signs of tiring. With 40 feet of leverage plus all the pressure my six-pound leader would allow, I successfully pulled him out of the current. He desperately tried to get back into it but to no avail. I now had to decide how to land the fish . . . 40 feet feet away. I inched him close to shore. Every time he flipped or flopped, I dragged him just a little bit further onto shore. Once on dry land, I was concerned that he would not flop back into the water, so with each additional wiggle I was able to drag him far enough onto shore. When satisfied that he would not escape, I laid down my rod on the cliff and tore down the path that led to the water's edge. There lay the steelhead. In the end, I never did get skunked on this run. What can I say. The Umpqua never fails.

The Spirit of the Northwest

For me, a part of good steelhead fishing is feeling comfortable in my surroundings. Maybe that's why I don't have much interest in taking trips to Alaska, British Columbia and Norway. It all feels so foreign and this causes me to feel distant from its essence. When we moved from Michigan to Oregon, it took the better part of a year to feel like the Northwest was home. Yes, I had caught plenty of steelhead that first year but it was as if I had caught them *someplace else.*

All this changed one wintry, sunny day in January. I drifted one of my favorite rivers, an enchanting coastal stream. I had gotten a late start that day but was content to take a half-day drift. This drift is custom-made for spinners as it is full of miniature pockets, pools, riffles, and tailouts. Midway through this spinner mecca, I approached one of the drift's major pools. I made progressively longer casts to sweep my spinner through the delightful frothing chop. Midway through one of these drifts, a steelhead grabbed the lure with a thunderous jolt.

It was one of the hardest takes I ever experienced. Being so startled by this strike, I was momentarily dazed. The fish immediately dashed down to the tail of the pool, then raced right up to its head as I scrambled to take up the slack. Then came the theatrics: sizzling runs, magnificent leaps and all that goes with it. Fresh from the ocean and with a high metabolism, this fish gave everything as it tried desperately to shake the hook. But because it had expended so much energy early on, it was easy to bring this incredible sea-run rainbow to the net.

After the whole ordeal was completed, I stood up. My senses seemed to open up as I heard the churning of fast water over rocks. I smelled the fresh air, admired the douglas firs, and enjoyed cheerful rays of sun that carved paths between towering trees, ending their journey on the water's surface. Somehow, the excitement and grandeur made the moment too valuable to continue fishing. I pulled the boat over to the shore positioning myself under a ray of sunshine and, while relaxing, took note of my own presence. I felt good about myself and appreciated my youth and strength. How good it was to be alive; to be drenched in sights, sounds and smells that were the essence of the Pacific Northwest. With a deep sigh, I felt a soothing energy flow from the river, forest and sky into my soul. Drifting rivers in search of steelhead – this is what I do. Living in Oregon – this is where I want to be. I had finally come home.

The author poses with a large steelhead from the McKenzie. Summer steelhead were introduced to the McKenzie about 15 years ago. Craig Rosner photo

Chapter 12

Trout

TROUT FISHING WITH SPINNERS RANKS AS one of my all-time favorite activities. For whatever big-fish glamour or sensationalism that is lacking is made up for in different and exciting ways. Steelhead fishing tends to be serious and intense. Trout fishing is more relaxed and casual. The often fast action of hooking many trout in succession makes hours seem like minutes. The savage strike of an aggressive fish renders an ultralight to a helpless state. And because resident trout tend to be more aggressive and less wary than large anadromous fish, we often see them chase and strike. Add this to a shore lunch and it produces a fishing addiction that is simply incurable. Yes, to fish an enchanting trout stream is a gift to all of mankind, one which should be preserved for future generations.

Before we delve into the world of trout, a couple of points need to be made that may provide some usefulness to you, the reader. First, if you plan to spend or already have spent considerable time with steelhead and spinners, the adaptation to trout and salmon will most likely be easily achieved. There are differences in habits and strategy, each of which is important to explore but there are more similarities than differences. In the steelhead chapters, we looked at every aspect of angling pursuit and explored each one in detail. In an effort to avoid needless repetition, the approach of the next two chapters is to concentrate on the uniqueness of the species considered. If your primary interest is salmon or trout to the exclusion of steelhead, I strongly suggest that you review the steelhead chapters. I feel there to be important information that will not be covered here but which nonetheless may provide valuable information and perspective.

The second point concerns the order of presentation of the next two chapters. It might be logical to think that a chapter on salmon should follow writings on steelhead.

After all, both groups of fish are large, anadromous, and frequent the same types of rivers. I really don't see it this way. A steelhead is a trout over and above everything else. Steelhead are more closely related to nonmigratory strains of other trout such as rainbow, cutthroats, and browns. In fact, a steelhead is nothing more than a migratory strain of rainbow. As fry and parr, the two are indistinguishable. From my point of view, salmon is something altogether different and should be treated as such. When I angle for trout and steelhead, I carry a certain type of mentality to the stream. When my attention turns to salmon, this mentality changes.

Three Survivors in a Changing World

Three species of trouts will be discussed here: rainbow, brown, and cutthroat. This choice is, only in part, a reflection of popularity. It also reflects catchability as well as current and future trends. The issue deserves exploration.

Before white man began to clumsily ravage the environment of North America, brook trout (actually a member of the char family) in the east and rainbow and cutthroat in the west monopolized our trout waters. Other species did and still do exist but the presence of brook, rainbow, and cutthroat distinguished them as the "big business" of the trout world. Furthermore, it was amazing as to just how far the ranges of these major species extended. Native brook trout could be found as far north as Hudson Bay and as far south as the state of Georgia. A small pond at the site of Thomas Jefferson's estate, Monticello, was used to hold trout. He would have his slaves capture live brook trout from nearby streams and keep them in his pond until ready to eat. The island of Manhattan was once an island rich in wildlife. Dozens of small streams held brook trout, some of which would migrate into New York Bay and return as "coasters."

At the southern tip of the island, a small lake, the "collect pond," was bubbling with brookies until overfished and polluted by Dutch settlers. They eventually filled the pond in 1829. This story is symbolic of the fate bestowed to the brook trout. But the continuous demise of the brook trout was not always a question of overfishing or the total destruction of habitat. It was also a result of the brook trout's inability to adapt to a wide range of harshly altered habitats.

Brown trout, imported from Europe, were introduced to Michigan and New York in the late 1800s. Although initially scorned by anglers because they were much more difficult to catch, the fraternity of trout fishermen came to accept and appreciate these European imports. The trend that began years ago continues today. Brook trout are in serious trouble. They are available but many of the quality waters especially those in Canada that hold thriving fisheries, are protected by stringent regulations that prohibit the use of anything but flies. Please don't misunderstand me. I applaud these conservation measures if they are our only means of preserving the unique fisheries that exist in the eastern Canadian provinces. But, for our purposes, it would seem pointless to study a fish that in many cases we can't even fish for.

The brown trout seems to have replaced the brookie in many of our eastern waters. The reason for its success can be answered in one word, *adaptability*. Consider, if you will, some astonishing facts about this trout. The brown's natural range extends latitudinally from Iceland to beyond Moscow and into the Asian provinces of Russia. Here is a trout which longitudinally extends from the Arctic region of Norway south into Iran, Lebanon, and Morocco. Geographically, the brown was initially found on nearly a quarter of the Earth's surface. Browns survive and multiply in the polluted and tepid streams of large urbanized areas. Fine specimens have been mysteriously found in freeway ditches and reports of fishery biologists in Colorado confirm the fact that large browns live in the city drainages of metropolitan Denver. Browns, as we have come to know them, are the strong survivors of the twentieth century. Browns have withstood intense fishing pressure for nearly 2,000 years. Records show that the Greeks and Romans fished browns heavily. This is an interesting point. It seems that the only way browns could have survived the heavy fishing pressure was through a Darwinian selection in which gullible strains were weeded out over the centuries, leaving one smart fish as the survivor. In sum, these bits of information lend a measure of logic to the brown's success and replacement of the brook trout in twentieth century America. The brown can withstand water temperatures up to 80°; the brookie has a maximum tolerance of 75°. The brown has a greater tolerance for pollution and various localized diseases; the brookie doesn't. The brown can multiply under a wide range of environmental conditions; the brookie can't. Browns can withstand intense fishing pressure; brookies can't. What this tells us is that the brown trout may be the trout of the future for an increasingly urbanized America. This does not mean we should write off brook trout. We must work hard to preserve this vanishing American. A brook trout is simply too beautiful a creation. Our future generations should have the opportunity to experience their uniqueness and awesome beauty in a natural setting.

From a practical point of view, the above thoughts lead me to believe that unless there is a major turnaround with regard to our national priorities, brook trout will become more and more protected with few quality opportunities for the spinner angler. It therefore seems wise to not consider them in our discussion. There is also an additional reason for omitting brook trout. If we compare catchability of the four major North American trouts (rainbow, brown, cutthroat, brook), there is a general consensus that brook trout are the easiest to catch. Thus, if you do well with the other three species, you shouldn't have any trouble with brookies.

While the eastern brook trout fishery has dwindled, the West Coast rainbow and cutthroat fisheries have hung on. This, I believe, can be accounted for by two factors. First, is the lack of dense population in areas like Northern California, Oregon, Wyoming, Idaho, and Montana. The second factor has to do with the abundance of cold mountain water which keeps the larger western rivers relatively clean, fast flowing, and, therefore, well-suited for trout. Rainbow, cutthroat (brown and brookies, too) abound in many rivers and multiply on their own. Although I now live in Eugene, Oregon, I grew up in northeastern Ohio. Trout were never a given. They were precious, expensive, temporary, and hard to get. For that reason, it will never fail to amaze me that I am always good for one or two trout when I take an hour to fish the Willamette River from the shores of downtown Eugene.

What about lake trout (mackinaw)? Don't they thrive in the Great Lakes, Finger Lakes, Ontario, Lake Tahoe, and other western lakes? Yes, but for the spinner fisherman, we have the problem of accessibility. Lake trout (also a char) prefer water temperatures in the low fifties. After the ice breaks, they can easily be caught but as the water warms up, they go deep. What this amounts to, in most cases, is three weeks of fishing in the spring. It is not fun and nearly impossible to effectively fish a spinner in 50 to 100 feet of water unless one employs a downrigger. This is not to say that practical lake trout fisheries don't exist. They do. The lakes and rivers of the Northwest Territories offer one opportunity as does the huge run of lakers that run up Michigan's Grand River every fall. But, here again, these fisheries are available to a small fraction of North American trout anglers.

The overall point is that rainbows, cutthroats, and browns are not only the strong survivors of our twentieth century civilization, but they are also the trout most accessible to the greatest number of anglers. With these thoughts, let's turn our attention to the pursuit of these three species.

One Thousand Varieties

One of the difficulties in writing about species distributed over a wide range of climates and terrains is that individual differences among the various strains within a species results in slightly different habits and angling techniques. The Kamloops trout of British Columbia lives in a climate much different from that of the redband trout of eastern Oregon. Yet, both are classified as rainbow trout. Similar differences exist among browns and cutthroats. Furthermore, trout of the same strain that are transplanted in different rivers, lakes and/or regions will, as a population, become adapted to that region over time, hence, a unique strain. Oregon's Hosmer Lake is a good example of this. The Atlantic salmon fishery that exists in that lake is the result of a program started in 1951 by the Oregon State Game Commission. Approximately ten thousand Atlantic salmon eggs were brought to the Wizard Falls Hatchery in central Oregon. The goal was to raise Atlantics for distribution in the surrounding Cascade Lakes. Only a few fish survived the four years necessary to mature and spawn. Each successive generation was more hardy than the previous. It took nine years of experimentation before a hardy strain was developed. The new environment of the salmon selected for certain characteristics that stood up to the various funguses, diseases, and parasites. What we ended up here with was a new "strain" of Atlantics. Is it then unreasonable to think that predatory habits might also be altered?

My conclusion is that any discussion of a species of trout that is well-distributed geographically should concentrate on general but not specific characteristics of the species as a whole. I like to view the same species of trout as being unique within its own watershed. Remain flexible in your approach. Just because you mastered the cutthroats of one river, you may encounter something totally different on a stream four miles down the road!

On this basis, we will discuss all aspects of spinner fishing for rainbows, browns, and cutthroats. The goal is to look at the major characteristics of each species and then translate this into spinner selection and technique.

Water Temperature

Although trout are considered to be delicate cold-water fish, they do have a surprisingly wide range of temperatures from which they can live and be angled from. There is no minimum water temperature that is necessary for rainbows, browns, and cutthroats to survive and/or be active in. They do quite well from 32° on up. Some fishermen believe that a cold harsh winter will do the trout in as evidenced by a mass of carnage that becomes evident when the ice melts on a lake. These occurrences are in part due to half-baked management of public or private lakes in which trout are exploited with all their dignity stripped. If trout are placed in a shallow lake or farm pond, thick ice from a harsh winter will reduce the amount of available oxygen because water-mass is reduced. The fish don't die of cold water. They die of suffocation. This is why conscientious owners of small ice-forming lakes typically punch a hole in the ice and add an aerator. You can bet that those trout will be hanging out at the ice hole, in part because of the warmer water but also because the water is better oxygenated.

A cold water temperature, in and of itself, is never a reason for trout not to bite. Now it is true that metabolism is lowered with lower temperatures. Trout do become less active but they do not hibernate or become inactive like bass. Trout that don't hit in cold water is a result of other relative factors that are putting the fish off the bite. Let's look at two sets of circumstances that would render a cold 38° favorable and unfavorable.

Case 1: It is late May in Colorado. The ice has broken on a mountain lake that was 33°. A week of unseasonably warm weather follows that raises the water temperature to 38°. The trout become very active and hit well.

Case 2: It is late November on an Oregon stream. The water temperature is 44° and the trout are biting well. A sudden cold front drops the temperature to 38° within 48

hours. The fish go totally off the bite. These typical scenarios show that no absolutes exist for a given temperature.

The same can be said for the upper temperature ranges also. We can have a cool 60° or a warm 60° depending on other relative factors. If this is the case, are there any general guidelines that will help determine whether a relative temperature is favorable or unfavorable? The preferred range of the species in consideration is somewhere between 52° and 65°. This will vary with each strain of each species. It is within this range that the trout feel most comfortable and are most active. If water within this range is available, the fish will find it. Two examples of this come to mind.

The author in action as he carefully brings in a large winter-run and finally nets it. Asa Pearl photo

A long-time personal friend lives on some property outside of Cleveland, Ohio. A beautiful spring-fed pond is his front yard. After several attempts at stocking rainbows in the lake, he became discouraged. A typical summer hot spell would drive the water temperature to above 75° and the fish would die. A cool spring feeds the pond at the northern end of the pond. He had a bulldozer dig out the shallow north end such that a pool was created that was substantially cooler than the rest of the pond. During the hot summer months, the rainbows stack up in this pool.

The second example is Lake Michigan. Nuclear power plants use the lake's water for cooling their reactors. When in operation, these facilities empty thousands of gallons of warm water back into the lake. It isn't long before the winter trout find this warm water. And it isn't long before fishermen find the fish.

A generalization can be made about trout and temperatures. *If we look at the 52° to 65° preferred range as a midpoint in a continuum, we can then say that trout will react favorably to temperature changes that tend toward this preferred range.* Thus, if water temperature rises from 34° to 43°, this will most likely have a favorable effect on fishing. Likewise, a change from 72° to 64° will also have a favorable effect. However, a change from 54° to 48° is likely to have a negative effect on fishing as is a change from 40° to 32°. As you can see, water temperature is often a relative factor that should be looked at in relation to the immediate past history of the watershed.

The author's long rod gives way to an Alaskan rainbow's incredible strength and stamina. David Davis photo

And what does a favorable temperature change do to the fish? It increases fish metabolism. If metabolism is higher, the trout become more active and they will feed more. Temperature changes that are directed *away* from the preferred range have a tendency to traumatize fish initially such that they lay low. For example, a trout can adjust well to a drop in temperature of 46° from 52° but initially the trout will have to adjust. However, trout do not seem to need to adjust to temperature changes in the direction of the preferred range. They seem to become energized and this translates into good fishing.

How does the above discussion tie into angling strategy? Very closely. It is almost always warmer during the day than at night. Warm air warms the water and cool air cools the water. Because the water is always warming and cooling, there will be certain times of the day where the water will be either warmer or cooler in the direction of the preferred temperature range. It is at these times when angling will be best. (This excludes extreme hot spells or cold fronts.)

Most anglers have been cliched into believing that trout fishing is best in the early morning or late evening. This is true in many cases but also untrue in many other cases. For example, a typical Michigan stream in August may cool to 60° at night. Naturally, a fishing day that begins at 5:00 a.m. when water is at its coolest is going to make trout more active since 60° is within their ideal range. When this water warms to 68° by noon, the fish become lethargic, taking little interest in anything. As a waning hot sun sets in the west, the waters begin to cool and the fish once again become active. This is a typical summer scenario but . . . simply does not apply for early spring, late fall, or for snow-melt streams that typically run much colder. Two examples demonstrate the point.

An angler in Pennsylvania rushes to be on the stream for the spring trout opener. The water temperature is 49° at 5:00 a.m. By 1:00 p.m. it has warmed to 54°. The fishing will most likely be better in the afternoon, not at dawn.

Oregon's McKenzie River, which I fish extensively, is yet another example of where first-one-on-the-river-catches-the-most-fish philosophy has no foundation. The McKenzie has as its source, melted snow from the Cascades. Even with our typical 80° to 90° summer days, the river never cools much past 58° or 60°. On a typical morning the water temperature will range from 52° to 54°. By 12:00 or 1:00 p.m., the temperature will be up to 57° or 58° and this is the time when I have my best rainbow and cutthroat fishing. This is because 57° or 58° is closer to the ideal or preferred range. Granted, I do catch trout at dawn when the water is 52° but rarely do I ever do as well as when the thermometer hits the upper fifties.

As suggested above, trout do not have a lower end temperature threshold. They can be angled from any water with a temperature down to 32°. Our concern is the upper limit, that point at which trout become lethargic. Here we have the problem of many strains distributed over a wide variety of geographical areas. We can make a few very general statements. Brown trout have the greatest tolerance for warm water. They can survive temperatures of up to 80° although they become lethargic at 75°. This is why they are so well-suited to the typical eastern stream that lacks large gushes of melting snow. Rainbow and cutthroat have less tolerance than browns. They would poach in 75° to 80° water. Some strains are in trouble at 70°. Cutthroat, in general, have a slightly greater tolerance than rainbow. Most strains of rainbow and cutthroat hit well in water that is up to 65°. Beyond this they become sluggish. But, once again, there are exceptions. The "redband" trout of eastern Oregon can withstand temperatures up to 78°. Whereas a Rocky Mountain rainbow might be lethargic, if not close to death in 70°, the redband rainbow will be quite active and negotiable.

Oxygen Needs

Of the three species considered, rainbows have the greatest need for well-oxygenated water. This is the main reason that when in rivers, rainbows can be found in riffles or fast-moving water, both of which tend to be better oxygenated than slack pools or eddies. Cutthroats have a more moderate need relative to rainbows. Where both species coexist, rainbows might be found in the fast upper white water sections of rivers while cutthroats will be more concentrated in lower river sections where the flow is gentler. Browns have even a lesser need for oxygen than do cutthroats. This makes them adaptable to rivers not normally thought of as being suitable for trout. While planted browns may not thrive in some of the polluted, low-oxygen, algae-ridden streams of the East and Midwest, they do survive and sometimes multiply.

Sunlight

Common belief has it that low light — that is, shaded areas dawn, dusk, and clouds — are all preferable to direct sunlight when fishing for trout. Here again, we must differentiate species and specific conditions. Contrary to what some anglers may think, sunlight can be a boon to trout fishing in certain circumstances. If not imminently endangered by predators, suffocating from a lack of oxygen, or spooked by anglers, a trout will first seek that temperature which best suits its biological needs. Other factors will aid in guiding a trout to this preferred range. Direct sunlight can be of benefit in helping trout to find this preferred range. For example, the afternoon angle of the sun may cast shadows along the shore of a tree-lined river. Certainly, the rainbows could hold in close to shore in $52°$ with the lower light providing cover but, instead, one finds them in direct sunlight in water that is slightly warmer due to the sun's direct rays. Since this preferred range is in the mid- to high fifties, they will opt for this water. Likewise, brown trout holding in a $32°$ Michigan river will hold in sunlight if available. Mind you, they are not sunning themselves. Rather, they are seeking that temperature which is closest to their preferred temperature range.

The typical trout scenario which most anglers are familiar with is one in which the sun comes out and the trout scatter or lay low. This usually happens under two circumstances. First, the trout are being spooked by angler presence. Second, the sun's rays are warming the water. Thus, the fish seek cooler deep holes or, in the case of a lake, simply go deeper. Now it is true that trout prefer the cover of reduced light and when water temperatures under cover and in direct sunlight are equal, the trout will opt for cover. But sunlight, first and foremost, should be seen in terms of what effect it has on water temperature in relation to the trout's preferred range.

Each of the three trouts considered has somewhat of a reputation for their like/dislike of sunlight. Rainbows are perhaps the most tolerant of direct sunlight. Much of this has to do with their needs for oxygen. If the water temperature is the same in all parts of the river, they will seek out that portion of the river that best suits their oxygen needs. Thus, it makes perfect sense that they would hold in direct sunlight if this is where needed oxygen-rich water can be found. Cutthroats have less of a need for oxygen. The result is that they have the luxury of seeking optimal cover under a wider variety of conditions. The illusion is given that they are less tolerant of sunlight than a rainbow. Not so. They simply can be more choosy. Browns are even more adaptable than cutthroats which means they can lie in slow deep holes or under structures. These places provide adequate oxygen and suitable water temperatures and at the same time maximize cover. This is one reason why browns are such strong survivors. Their needs as a trout are far less than some of the other species. Rainbows and cutthroats can't afford to be so choosy. They need cooler water and more oxygen. The result of these comparisons

again leaves us with the conclusion that browns hate sunlight. In my opinion, it is their greater adaptability that is allowing them to seek optimal cover. If given a choice, all other factors being favorable, any trout prefers the sanctuary of low light or cover.

Water Surface

Water surface can play a large role in determining whether trout will hit or not. In low light conditions, the smoothness of a river's tailout or the stillness of a lake will not inhibit a trout to hit. The problem is that the majority of our fishing occurs during the day, a time when maximum summertime lighting renders trout vulnerable to predators. The slight chop of a lake or the riffles of a river do wonders in providing enough security such that trout maintain an aggressive posture. If given the choice during daylight hours, I will always fish water that has a break to the surface. The amount of break to the surface is not as critical as having some minimal break. When planning a day of trout fishing on a lake, I may think twice about working the shorelines if the water is calm or, if there is a slight wind, I will seek out the shore that is *least* protected.

Putting It Altogether

Any type of holding water chosen by trout is the summation of the four factors discussed. There are, of course, other minor factors to consider such as wind direction, water height, etc. (see Chapter 6), but rarely will they have greater importance than water temperature, oxygen, sunlight, and water surface. Although oxygen content cannot be measured, we do know that turbulent water will create more oxygenation. For water temperature, all we need is a simple water thermometer. Lighting and water surface are easily observed. With this information and a bit of knowledge about the habits of a particular species, we can then make intelligent decisions about where to find the trout.

One of the criticisms I have of fly-fishing and spin-fishing literature is that there is far too much emphasis placed on flies, lures, and casting techniques. There is no question that the right bait presented in the proper way is needed but, in order to successfully employ a technique, you have to know where the fish are, too. The best lure cannot catch fish where they don't exist. Our famous McKenzie River here in Oregon is a perfect example of my point. During any given season, I am witness to anglers who display magnificent skills as evidenced by pinpoint casting, perfectly tied flies, and beautifully built lures. And yet, I watch many of these same anglers fish the wrong water at the wrong times. I see them pass up water that has yielded great numbers of magnificent trout (steelhead, too). They are fishing randomly — in a way which only by chance is matched to the right water. Wouldn't it be better if they could know what to look for and then use their techniques in those places where they know the fish will be?

The environment does not lie! Water thermometers always tell the truth. And you can always know if the sun is out or where the broken water surface is. Add these environmental factors together and they are a dead giveaway about where the trout are and what they will hit.

Buy a thermometer and take notes on water temperature, lighting, surface, and the type of water you angled your fish from. Within a short period of time you will see patterns develop. That is, when the water is of a certain temperature, the sky has a certain amount of lighting, and the water surface has a certain degree of smoothness or choppiness, the trout will most always respond in the same way by going to the same types of places and by hitting the same spinners.

When I fish one of the trout rivers near my home, I know within 30 seconds of the start of my day where the trout will be. I take a temperature reading, look into the sky, and I'm on my way. I will check the water temperature every hour or so while at the same time being constantly aware of lighting. Thus, I know where to fish and where *not* to fish. This means that I can cover far more water too because I don't waste time in the unproductive spots. I fish with confidence because I know what to use when and where. When you fish with confidence, you catch more fish.

Holding Water in Rivers

Rainbows, cutthroats and browns have certain basic habits in terms of where they will hold in a typical river. All of these habits are a result of the biological needs discussed above. Without going into the biological whys of each behavior, let's discuss a few of the basics.

All three species, unless very large, will seek slow-moving or slack water when the temperature of the water dips below 50°. In water of 52° and up, rainbows become "riffle" or "fast-water" trout. One will generally find them in either fast tailouts, riffles, or runs with a medium speed. If this water is not available, they will opt for water that provides the best combination of oxygenation and cover. Browns and cutthroats will sometimes hold in riffles although they are most frequently found in these places prior to spawning. Browns will hold in a riffle very close to a structure or deep hole/drop-off. In many cases, browns and cutthroats are more oriented toward cover. They like the protection of rocks, logs, undercut banks or any structure from which they can dart out and seize a minnow or insect. Rainbows are most negotiable in sunlight if the water has a broken surface. When holding in slick sunlit tailouts, they tend not to hit well. Browns and cutthroats are less tolerant of sunlight often going deep or seeking refuge by a shaded shoreline. Browns are night feeders, too. They can be caught in total darkness with a spinner. In fact, some of the largest browns I have ever caught were taken off of piers in Lake Michigan in the early a.m. hours. As with rainbows, a broken surface is preferable for browns or cutthroats except during extreme low-light conditions. Brown trout are the most sensitive to angler presence. In general, these trout are the most wary. Rainbows are less wary and cutthroats are even less so.

As browns and cutthroats have similar preferences for holding water, either is very compatible with rainbows within a given river system. Where the browns/cutthroats may hold in the slower lower river sections, the rainbows will dominate the faster upper river sections. In a particular pool, the rainbows will hold in the tail or just below the break in the white frothy water. The browns/cutthroats will be further downstream in deeper water, off to the side of the pool, or stationed at a drop-off. Although I am sure there are cases where the two exist together, it would be interesting for me to personally see how cutthroats and browns would distribute themselves within the same river system.

Lake Strategy

Trout fishing in lakes always seems to be more of a challenge. In a large expanse of water with little definition, it can be difficult to determine where the fish are. However, there are a few basics that can help to determine when to fish and where.

When ice breaks in the spring, the trout will head for the surface and to the shore in order to place themselves in the warmest water. This is also a time when trout will start to feed voraciously.

After waters warm and assume their typical summer temperatures, trout are quite negotiable in smooth or still water during low light, dawn or dusk. They often seek out small fish or insects in shallow sandy bays or in weed beds. The edge of drop-offs or rocky shoals are also prime areas to consider. During the daytime hours, however, this changes. Except for when the ice breaks, under clouds or in choppy water, still-water fishing is often nonproductive. When fishing during the day, I like to find water that has a broken surface and if none is to be found, I may think twice about fishing. When fishing a large lake, the instinct of many anglers is to find a protected bay, one which will increase personal comfort but this is often done at the expense of good fishing. Trout in lakes need protection if they are to expose themselves. Low light gives them needed security. The only other way to get it is through a broken water surface. Otherwise, they go deep and lay low. When fishing trout in summer, I try to find a rocky shore or one with structure. True, the boating can be rough. One often spends more time maneuvering the boat than fishing but this is where the trout, especially the large ones, will be most active. When with a partner under such conditions, the person running the motor trolls and the other man casts.

The positive effects of a broken surface cannot be overestimated. We have a number of man-made reservoirs here in Oregon that hold good numbers of trout. About three or four times a year, I like to troll the lakes with a small spinner. It is an easy, relaxing type of fishing that is a nice change of pace from the intense and rigorous steelhead fishing that I do all year. This type of fishing also brings back memories of Canada and the type of trolling we typically did for walleyes, pike, and smallmouth. The trout are very predictable when trolling. With a slight breeze, they move in close to shore and near the surface. When the wind stops, they go deeper or out into the middle of the lake. So when trolling, I head for the shores if the wind kicks up. If it dies down, I head for the middle of the lake, decrease my trolling speed, and fish deeper.

Inlets and outlets are excellent places to look for trout when fishing a lake. Trout will gravitate to a stream that empties into a lake for its cooler water and/or for the potential food that will be washed into the lake. The outlets of lakes are also natural havens for trout cruising for small fish and other food sources. One might say that trout like portions of a lake where there is the greatest flow or most activity.

Surf fishing for trout is probably one of the most misunderstood types of fishing. A lot of anglers have this idea that the further you wade into the water and the farther you cast your bait, the better the fishing will be. This belief is probably instilled from the sight of saltwater surf fishermen whose massive rods are built to cast lures and bait up to 600 feet. When a shoreline is calm and lacks wave activity, it is then important to cast far into the surf. The fish will be holding in the deeper water and won't come in close unless it is spring and the ice has just broken. However, when waves are rolling into the beach and the water is choppy, the trout will practically be at your feet and I'm not necessarily talking about small ones either. I have caught five- to 12-pound browns that were within 15 feet of the edge of the water. The trout are here for a good reason. Small fish, which for protection stay close to shore, lose control in the pounding surf. Various items dislodged from the sand wash into the surf where eager trout snap them up. The sound of the surf and the broken surface give the trout a shield of protection from which they will lower their guard and feed aggressively.

Cloud cover will, to some extent, compensate for the lack of a pounding surf or increase activity in an already active surf. When surf fishing the shores of the Great Lakes, there have been times when the sky has scattered cloud cover. I watch the clouds closely, trying to position myself under a precious cloud and it pays off. The trout will look for this cover and become more aggressive under it.

Sea-Run Cutthroat

The sea-run cutthroat, one of many subspecies, is an anadromous cutthroat that is found along the west coast of the United States. With a range from Northern California to Prince William Sound in Alaska, this particular cutthroat is singled out for two reasons. First, they are a very unique trout in that they spend a good portion of their adult lives in either the saltwater estuary or ocean proper before ascending their natal streams to spawn. In this regard, they are neither solely a river trout nor open-water trout. They are taken in many different types of waters. Second, they are a trout that has a very faithful and growing following. They do deserve some individual attention.

Returning adult sea-runs start entering the tidal estuaries in July. A good number have pushed well into the lowest riffles above tidewater by September and early October. As the initial heavy rains of the season swell rivers, the sea-runs will push upstream. Here they rest in relatively slack water — quiet pools and eddies waiting for their eggs and milt to ripen. When the time is right, the cutthroats will make a final run into small tributaries of the main river where they will spawn. Spawning occurs between December and February. Post-spawners will rest quietly for a few days and then start to feed once again. They quickly restore their dissipated strength and recover weight lost in the rigors of spawning. They will slowly make their way downstream until they reach the bay or ocean by mid-spring. They will then return in the fall.

When my wife and I moved to Oregon, I was told that while sea-runs were easy to catch, it was finding them that was the biggest challenge. During my first fall and winter of Northwest fishing, I caught dozens of sea-runs while fishing for salmon and steelhead but never thought much of it. They seemed easy to catch and were very plentiful. Late in

the steelhead season, I was talking to *Salmon Trout Steelheader* magazine editor Frank Amato about sea-runs. He asked if I had caught any. I then told him in a very casual way that I had caught somewhere around a hundred and twenty five. He gave me a look as if I had insulted him and then exclaimed, "A hundred and twenty five?!" Half-shocked, I replied, "At least that many, so what's the big deal?" Since that initial season, I haven't come close to matching the quantity caught my first year. This, in part, is a result of the rivers I fished then versus the rivers I fish now. It also must be said that that first year was an exceptional year for sea-runs. In any event, what I realized is that I was doing something right. I have a perspective on what makes for good sea-run fishing. I would like to pass it on.

This springer took a small "trout standard" while the author was pursuing cutthroat on the lower McKenzie. Jed Davis

Tidewater fishing for sea-runs can be very difficult. The river is slow-moving and undefined. Therefore, unless one has considerable experience within a particular tidewater area, it is almost impossible to determine where the fish will be holding — if anywhere in particular. Other conditions also make for difficult angling. The stream bed is wide and open. There are no riffles or broken surfaces that provide protection. The result is that fish can be spooky. For this reason, I limit my tidewater fishing to environmental conditions that will give the sea-runs the greatest amount of security such that they will maintain an aggressiveness necessary for them to strike. First, sea-runs should be fished on the incoming tide. Fishing seems best from three hours before high tide to one hour after. Early morning or late evening fishing can be meaningless unless these periods coincide with high tide. Second, I will only fish tidewater if I know that it will be a cloudy/rainy day. My best luck takes place on days with a peach-fuzz drizzle or intermittent rain. I certainly would prefer to fish during a sunny Indian summer day but the strong sun has a tendency to cause fish to be skittish. I most always seem to do well when the cloudy/rainy conditions exist. This leads me to believe that finding the sea-runs isn't the difficult part as much as it is finding the optimal set of conditions from which to pursue them.

Once above tidewater, the strategy changes. Tides do not figure into determining optimal times to fish. Under these circumstances, low light conditions are preferable. This is because sea-runs will often hold in slack pools or close to shore. This type of water has no broken surface. Therefore, the fish lay low in sunny weather. If fishing under sunny skies, I look for places in my drifts that offer especially good cover — undercut banks, boulders, overhanging branches and brush, and especially riffles. As for the latter, I would say that a good percentage of my sea-runs come from riffles. In fact, if I know that it is going to be sunny all day, I opt for the drift that has the best and most abundant riffles.

Spinner Presentation

In Chapter 5, I outlined in detail how the spinner is best presented to steelhead. In regard to trout, I would add the following comments.

Sizes 0, 1 and 2 are the most commonly used spinner sizes. As I pointed out earlier, it is difficult if not impossible to fish these sizes for a slow blade-spin. Pulsations are much less defined than on the larger No. 3, 4 and 5 spinners. I therefore do not concern myself with blade speed. I largely ignore it. Instead, I fish the spinner as a whole, trying to control the speed of the entire lure through the water.

Speed of retrieval is another important concern. A general rule (that has its exceptions) applies here: *In slower water, a faster retrieve is used. In faster water, a slower retrieve is used.* I have always regarded fast retrieves in slow water as an added exciter. If a spinner is swimming very quickly through a predator's territory, instinct tells the trout to "chase." If this same spinner goes through at a slow speed, it almost seems unnatural. It also gives the trout time to examine the bait. In fast water, the current takes care of the speed. Quite often, a trout will follow the spinner downstream and strike once it has swung into the current. The trout may also follow the spinner on the retrieve for quite a distance. By using a fast retrieve in fast water, a trout may then not be given adequate time to follow and/or strike.

Searching for trout and steelhead on the North Santiam in Oregon. Jed Davis photo

If fishing a deep hole of four feet or more, a bottom presentation may become imperative. Otherwise, it should not be a major concern. Hungry trout are extremely aggressive. They are also fast swimmers. If a negotiable trout is lying on the bottom, a lure passed three feet above his nose can be seen, chased, and attacked. This does not mean that bottom presentations are not always a smart idea. A good spinner fisherman will always try to work that spinner close to the bottom. However, it isn't always necessary. If I can only get within three feet of the edge of a sunken log under which trout hold, I know that my cast spinner has a good chance of inducing the strike of a trout that is no closer than five feet away. The point here is not to get discouraged or lose confidence if you can only get so close.

As noted by Les Johnson in his book *Sea-Run*, cutthroat have a following trait that can drive an angler crazy. They will sometimes follow a lure right to the boat without striking. Throw the lure out and they will do it again. Browns do the same thing on occasion. How do you get these teasers to strike? One method is by changing lures. Use of a different color/finish spinner can do the trick. I have depended on another method as noted by Johnson. I call it "feinting." When a cutthroat or brown can be seen following a spinner, stop your retrieve and let the spinner drop for a couple of seconds. Then start your retrieve once again. This is an effective method at getting reluctant cutthroats and browns to hit.

Feinting is also very effective in teasing trout out of hard-to-reach areas. For example, I may suspect that trout are lying well underneath a log at the river's edge that has not yet sunk. I cannot cast under the log . . . only to the edge of the log. To insure maximum visibility to potential quarries, I will cast to the edge of the log and, instead of retrieving immediately, I will let the spinner flutter to the bottom. The flip-flop of the blade on its way down makes for a lot of flash. (Throw a metal can opener into a swimming pool and see how much flash is produced.) This technique has accounted for many beautiful trout. One of my biggest browns was an 11-pounder that came from Michigan's Betsie River. This river has turned out some monster 15- to 20-pound browns. Anytime you see sunken logs or log jams, it's a sign that big browns may be near. On one particular October day in 1978, I cast my spinner to the edge of a log. I repeated with many casts until the entire length of the log was covered. I then decided to feint. On the first cast, Wham-O! I felt a solid thud which at first I thought was a branch. Well, it was as long as a branch, but more closely resembled a beautiful brown trout. Feinting on the cast will cost you a few lures. However, once you've hooked a few nice trout, the lost spinners will seem to be a minor sacrifice.

Spinner Size

Because sizes 0, 1 and 2 spinners are the most effective sizes for most trout fishing situations, it is not uncommon to find oneself in a situation where tiny trout are becoming somewhat of a nuisance. The sight of a four-inch trout on a No. 2 spinner is at first amusing but quickly becomes annoying if the little guys persist. This is when I go to a larger spinner.

The psychology of "use a big lure, catch a big fish" kind of works . . . sorta. If conditions are such that all the trout are hitting, then this old adage has some merit. For example, if I were fishing for rainbows at dusk and activity was constant, this would be telling me that the big fish were on the feed. In an effort to get by the smaller fish, I might go to a large No. 4 spinner. However, if you have a situation where small cutthroats are hitting well in bright sunlight, the larger spinner may spook the more desirable larger fish. Only the small spinner will get them to hit. The largest steelhead trout that I have hooked to date was an estimated 20- to 24-pound job taken on Oregon's McKenzie. My records and experience indicate that had I been using a spinner larger than a No. 2, the fish would have either ignored the spinner or been spooked. A good general rule to follow is that the brighter the lighting, the shallower the water, the clearer the water, and the slower the water, then the smaller the spinner. The point here is that, unless the special circumstances like those alluded to above exist, lure size should not be determined solely by fish size. *Environmental conditions are much more of an important consideration in determining spinner size.*

Spinner Color and Finish

I face one major problem in writing a section on the best colors and finishes to use for trout. That is, **everything works!** As long as a spinner is functioning properly and the angler knows how to fish where and when, I can't imagine a combination of color and finish that wouldn't work at least marginally for most trout in most locations. This rather startling statement is testimony to the effectiveness of the spinner. It is a remarkable lure, one which inventors would be hard-pressed to beat.

Yes, there are shades of spinner effectiveness. Serious anglers have definite preferences in terms of colors and finishes used on spinners. Let's first take a look at finish. Silver-like finishes seem to be favored in low light — that is, clouds, dawn, dusk. Darker or duller finishes such as brass, black oxide or purposely-tarnished brass are favored during the daytime. Although silver-bladed spinners outsell brass, copper and black oxide by a wide margin, I personally have much greater success with the latter, to the point where I rarely use silver anymore for trout. I don't think silver's added flash adds any appeal, especially when fishing the typical clear summer river. In fact, I feel that silver spooks a lot of would-be trout. My approach of the last several years has been to create spinners that give presence but do not produce the sharp contrast that has traditionally been the goal of manufacturers. By presence I mean that I want the fish to know that the spinner is there but I don't want to startle the trout. This is accomplished in two ways. In one strategy, I try to have my spinner blend in with the surroundings as much as possible by keying off colors that are created by the aquatic environment. Another direction has been the creation of spinners that absorb all light, therefore giving off no flash whatsoever. My "McKenzie Dark" with its black blade and tarnished brass body has been a wonder lure when fished in bright sunlight in temperatures above 52°. I believe that its success is due, in part, to its producing presence without contrast. The fish are totally unintimidated but at the same time curious! *When you have developed a bait for a set of circumstances in which you make fish aware of the bait's presence without spooking the fish, you have then created the ultimate spinner* (see "Threshold of Attraction," Chapter 2).

This leads to a very important point about trout spinners. In order to be an effective designer of spinners, you must free yourself from judging spinners on looks. Just because a spinner looks good, this does not mean that it will work well. This sounds very simplistic but who hasn't looked into his tackle box, put a shiny new lure to the light and then said to his partner, "Doesn't that look just great?" Go look at any sporting goods shelf. What do you see? Flashy spinners with all sorts of cerise (bright fluorescent red) beads, and neon-colored adornments. People won't buy them if they don't look great. That's basic marketing. But are they the best spinners to buy?

I am a manufacturer of fishing tackle. Two years ago, I decided to seriously consider adding a line of spinners. I took some of my very plain spinners to a friend to ask his opinion. He had been in the tackle business for 20 years and can tell fairly quickly whether something has potential. I proudly showed him my spinners and exclaimed, "These really work!" He shook his head and replied, "I believe you and I know you do well, but I must be frank in saying that no distributor would ever take them. They'll never sell."

I am reminded of the day I discovered the value of tarnished brass. Up until this day, I was one who believed in a sparkling new spinner. I put a rag and polish to any spinner that had the slightest bit of tarnish. On this particular day, I had lost all of my No. 2 brass spinners. Unknowingly, I looked down into my tackle box and realized that if I wanted to use the No. 2 brass, it was going to be a disgusting looking model that was lying on the bottom tray. In fact, I had reminded myself to throw it out the day before but had forgotten. Feeling like my day was ruined, I put it on. On the first cast, I hooked a nice trout. On the second cast, I hooked a summer steelhead that twisted off. I moved downstream. The next cast produced a thunderous jolt which ten minutes later turned out to be a 13½-pound summer steelhead. I moved down to the next run and bang! A nine-and-a-half-pound steelhead. No, a tarnished No. 2 won't produce action like this every time out or every fifth trip out. But needless to say, this thrilling experience significantly changed my orientation toward spinners.

When we speak of color on trout spinners, it is usually in reference to tubing placed on hook shanks and pressure-sensitive tape that is adhered to blades. Colored beads may also be used. However, I personally don't use beads because they take up valuable space on the spinner shaft that can be used for weighting with heavy metal beads. When using small No. 0, 1 and 2 spinners, we want to maximize casting distance by maximizing weight.

The typical color scheme in store-bought spinners uses *contrast* as a means of attraction. In other words, if trout see a spinner that is highly contrasted against the underwater environment, the trout's attention will be drawn to the lure, thus creating the greatest possibility of a strike. This philosophy has merit but it is very overdone. High contrast can be valuable in low light, murky water, or cold-water conditions. My personal use of high contrast spinners is very limited. I use the typical fluorescent red-oranges or yellows when my rivers are still high and cloudy from winter runoff. I also use these colors when water temperature is below 48° or 50°. In this case, trout metabolism will be below its peak level. The high contrast is an inducer that will excite a semi-lethargic fish into striking.

When the rivers have cleared and water temperatures are at their typical levels, it is rare that I will use a high contrast spinner. During these conditions, there are two basic strategies that can be used. The first strategy, as discussed above, involves creating *presence without contrast*. I believe the spinner to be a great attention-getter. The action and the sonic attraction are so great that even the dullest, darkest and dirtiest spinner will catch the attention of fish. Therefore, you don't need much to get a fish to take note of your offering. This has led to the development of spinners that blend in well with the surroundings. If the water has a greenish cast or if algae or green plants coat the river's bottom, I may use green tapes and tubings. If I am fishing a slate-bottomed river in New York State, I might use dark-red or brown adornments. If a sharply-angled sun is shining directly into the eyes of holding river fish, I may employ golds to match the sun's rays. In these cases, I am creating an attention-getter by keying in on what's already present.

This strategy may seem to be a contradiction to my whole theory of "spinner as attractor" as stressed in earlier chapters. In those chapters, I stressed the importance of creating the most attention-provoking spinners: "How much glitter and flash can the fish stand before it is turned off?" The implication here is that we should always strive for contrast. In fact, the typical winter steelhead spinner does just that. It creates tremendous contrast. So, if we are using the same theory, why create a spinner that blends in well with surroundings? If anything, wouldn't this decrease attraction?

The author admires a buck taken from shore. Asa Pearl photo

From my point of view, I am trying to achieve the same thing. I am simply going about it differently. Instead of keying on differences, I am keying on similarities and using these similarities to bring out color. Let's take a typical example. Imagine a girl with green eyes. When she wears a green sweater, the green in her sweater makes her eyes look more green, or her eyes catch the attention of more people. Likewise, when I use a brass spinner with fluorescent kelly green adornments against the background of green-hued water, the water color heightens the presence of the green in my spinner. I am therefore creating tremendous presence.

One may then ask, "Why use total contrast in some cases and presence without contrast in other cases?" This has to do with metabolism. When trout or steelhead are in waters below their preferred high metabolism range, something very startling is needed to excite them into striking. Strong reds, yellows and flashy metallics are the best provokers. Yes, the fish become startled or excited but since their metabolism is low, they are not excited or startled to the point where they spook. Rather, they are triggered into an aggressive response. The typical trout or summer steelhead that is angled for in warmer waters has a very high metabolism. They too will become startled or excited by reds, yellows, and metallics but, because they are so alert, their level of excitement goes beyond being aggressive. That is, they become somewhat "hysterical" such that they excite themselves right out of an aggressive mood. It is sort of like the athlete who loses his cool. He becomes so aggressive or wound up that he can't do his job on the field. By matching colors — green with greens, gold with golds, etc. — one is creating a presence that is attention-getting but which does not sharply contrast such that the level of excitement becomes too great.

Another strategy incorporates the colors of fishes, crustaceans, and insects that the trout typically feed on. The idea here is that the trout becomes conditioned to striking objects of a certain color which it has learned to feed on. The introduction of that same color triggers a response based on habit. For example, if trout are feeding on bright red-orange crayfish (very abundant here in the Northwest) a spinner that employs this same color on its blade and hook shank may trigger a response to strike. I am very confident that this is partially responsible for the success I have achieved with my black-bladed spinner. Most of a trout's diet in rivers are objects that are small, dull and dark. This spinner, with its rotating black blade, very much gives the impression of a caddis, nymph, leech, or beetle when in the water.

For me to suggest colors that work well for a particular species or for trout in general would be to base these statements on the experience in my rivers and lakes. There are thousands of rivers and lakes that I will never fish. Each should be treated as a unique body of water. Yellows, reds, golds, and blacks are popular but don't ever discount greens, blues, or purples.

Ready-Made Trout Spinners

Here again, I would be doing a disservice by suggesting the use of one brand of spinners over another. All spinners, if spinning properly, work. What's more important is finding sizes, finishes, and colors that match your particular set of circumstances as discussed above. There are, however, some general points that apply to all trout spinners. These need to be dealt with seriously if you want to optimize the effectiveness of your technique.

Throughout this book, I have continually encouraged the use of the French-type blade. In fact, all of my techniques are based on the assumption that this blade will be used. When it comes to salmon and steelhead fishing, I stand by my assertion that this blade is unbeatable. This is because it is the most versatile, the most dependable, and the easiest to control for the slow blade-spin that is so deadly on salmon and steelhead. With the smaller spinners that are typically used for trout, controlling for slow blade-spin is nearly impossible. Therefore, we don't concern ourselves with this aspect of technique. For this reason, I will never say that use of a French blade is imperative or that it even makes a difference. What I will say is that your chosen spinner must spin dependably and on command. If you have to yank on the rod tip to start it or if you have to reel it quickly in order to keep it spinning, then you are going to miss a lot of fish. The best spinner is one that spins so dependably that you never concern yourself with whether it is working properly. Unfortunately, most manufacturers of spinners are not spinner fishermen. They are businessmen. The goal is a pretty spinner, a catchy name, appealing packaging, and an attractive price. They are banking on the fact that you won't know or care if the spinner is functioning properly. If I go into a store and consider various brands of spinners, perhaps only one in three is properly designed. That is why it is so important to experiment until you find the good brands.

Take a few moments. Does the blade start spinning immediately upon retrieve? Will the blade consistently spin at a slow speed? Is there enough weight to cast an adequate distance and maintain proper depth in a fast current?

Hooks are a very crucial part of a spinner. Quality wide-bend trebles as described in Chapter 2 are so important. Cheap hooks with a dull point simply do not penetrate and hold. When a steelhead or salmon takes a spinner, they take it solidly. You can then sometimes get away with dull points on the hook. Trout often make tenative passes with quick nips. Only a good hook will get these fish. When you land a beautiful three-pound trout, you will soon forget that you paid an extra thirty cents for a spinner with a quality hook.

If your interest in spinner fishing is of a more casual nature such that you don't have the time or interest in making your own spinners from scratch, why not consider customizing store-bought spinners? It is very simple. For example, you may find a spinner that, aside from the hook, you really like. Buy some pre-formed spinner shafts, some good hooks, and rebuild the spinner with nothing more than a needle-nose pliers. Experimenting with different color pressure-sensitive tapes is easily done. Most spinners have a plain metal blade or a piece of tape adhered to the outside of the blade. In the case of the latter, this can be easily peeled off. You may want to try some red, green, or yellow on the blade. Solid vinyls and prism-tapes are readily available. Place a piece on the inside of the blade and you are on your way.

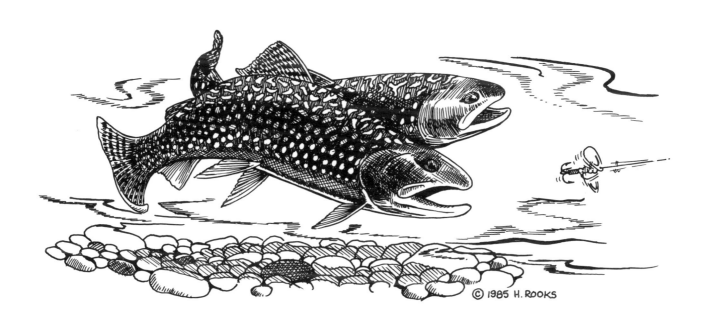

© 1985 H. ROOKS

Chapter 13

Salmon

WHILE SALMON FISHING IS VERY SIMILAR TO steelhead fishing, there are important differences in technique. A knowledge of these differences is often the key to success. The purpose of this chapter is to concentrate on the uniqueness of salmon fishing relative to steelhead fishing. As I mentioned in the trout chapter, there is a lot of information in the steelhead chapters that is also important for salmon fishing so if your interest is in salmon to the exclusion of steelhead, I would advise you to at least glance at the steelhead chapters.

Two species of salmon will be discussed here — coho and chinook. The decision to concentrate on these species is based on abundance, distribution and popularity. Not only are coho and chinook found from central California north to Alaska, but they are also now widely distributed in the Great Lakes. With the declining Atlantic salmon resource in Maine and the eastern Canadian provinces, there has also been talk of planting these rivers with coho salmon. There is absolutely no question that coho and chinook are the most sought after species of salmon.

Sockeye, pink, and chum salmon are well distributed throughout many portions of Alaska (also in a few places in the Pacific Northwest) but then how many anglers have the opportunity to fish Alaska? I have fished Alaskan sockeye, pink and chum. In fact, if I had my choice, I would prefer to fish for sockeye over any of the other species. But during the times I fished them, they were so plentiful and easy to catch that it was difficult to determine what spinner techniques worked because everything seemed to work. This is not to say that these three species are at times and in various situations always eager to strike or plentiful to the point where you can walk on them. Much has been written, for example, about sockeyes that show a total lack of interest in lures of any kind. I simply was never in a situation where a great deal of skill was needed to hook sockeyes, pinks or

chums. In this regard, they remain somewhat of a mystery to me. My trips to Alaska have been to fairly inaccessible locations at the very peak of the season when good fishing was assured. Therefore, it seems that the only way that I could develop a real sense for these fish is by living in locations where they are readily available. In my case at least, spending an extended amount of time in Alaska, let alone moving there, seems highly unlikely.

Although called a salmon, the Atlantic salmon is really a trout, more closely linked to steelhead as noted by author Trey Combs in *Steelhead Flyfishing and Flies*. Both species have very similar life cycles and behavioral characteristics. I personally regard Atlantics as an "eastern steelhead" and steelhead as "western Atlantics."

Aside from the above issue, the question may be asked as to why I have not considered Atlantic salmon in this book? Believe me, I would like to. The problem is angling restrictions. Virtually all great Atlantic salmon water in North America, Canada and Scandinavia is restricted to "flies only." While there is some opportunity to spin fish in Iceland and Scotland, this state of affairs does not lend itself to the development of any spinner technique. The door is slammed shut in 85% of the cases.

A couple of years ago, I looked into the possibility of taking an Atlantic salmon trip. I was, however, uncompromising on one point. That is, I wanted to do it *my* way. I must have written 20 letters explaining my desire to fish for Atlantics with spinning tackle. I became very discouraged and somewhat annoyed by the snobbery of the fly-fishing elite that truly believe that they are above all other forms of fishing. Iceland seemed to be the only worthwhile possibility—albeit a very good one. Iceland's policy is that on most rivers, you can either fish with a fly or a worm. On a few rivers, lures are permitted. Here was an opportunity but at $4,500 a shot, I suspect that I would be surviving on kosher hot dogs and peanut butter in the coming years. I find it rather sad that such a marvelous fish so rich in angling history has been delegated to the wealthy class. Nature's bounty is the gift of all mankind. I will never buy the idea that the right to fish should be determined by the pocketbook. On the other hand, there is good reason for the angling restrictions on Atlantic salmon. Contrary to what Lee Wulff would like to believe, spinners are generally much more effective Atlantic salmon lures than are flies. In the few places where both flies and spinners are permitted for the angling of Atlantic salmon, the spinners have outfished the flies fairly convincingly. Thus, the "flies only" restriction is, in part, a conservation measure designed to protect the fishery. I suppose that in the end this is more important but I still don't think that this fully justifies excluding the spin fisherman.

There is one very promising development on the horizon concerning Atlantic salmon. As you may be aware, Lake Ontario and its tributaries once boasted the world's only natural freshwater Atlantic salmon fishery. Dams, poaching and pollution totally destroyed the massive runs of Atlantics to 40 pounds that once ascended to the Lake Ontario tributaries in upstate New York. It has always been a dream to bring back an Atlantic salmon fishery and, apparently, it's starting to work. Although in its infancy, the first run of grilse (precocious "jacks" much like salmon and steelhead) is on the verge of ascending the streams. One of the field testers of my tackle manufacturing firm has caught dozens of Atlantic salmon in Lake Ontario while trolling for Pacific salmon during this past summer, 1984. This is an excellent sign that the strain of fish planted can survive in good numbers. As New York State is generally opposed to the "fly only" concept, we could be on the verge of creating an Atlantic salmon fishery that will give spin fishermen the chance they always deserved.

A Strategy Suited for Salmon

I earlier alluded to the idea that when going after salmon, I use a different mentality in my approach. While knowledge of holding water and spinner techniques are very important, I am of the opinion that nothing is more important as knowing *when* to be on the river. With the exception of spring chinook, picking your salmon days is just as important as everything else combined. Salmon behave according to a finite genetic clock. We want to go after the fish when they are fresh and most willing to bite. In order to make our effort worthwhile, we want to be able to predict when the fresh fish will be coming in, where they will hold, and when is the best time to go after them. This will be the primary emphasis of this chapter.

Years ago, the abundance of salmon in the Pacific Northwest was so great that good fishing could be had by anyone who had minimal angling skills. This is no longer the case . . . in fact, far from it. In the Great Lakes states, the salmon programs have been a tremendous success. Massive plants, successful natural reproduction and a high adult survival rate among smolts has produced one of the great success stories of modern times. Many rivers abound with salmon in staggering numbers. But there are also problems in these areas that can make stream fishing a real challenge. One of these problems is the population density of these areas. The Great

Lakes states boast one-third of the fishing licenses issued in the United States in any one year. When the salmon are in, large numbers of anglers are right on their tails. The second problem is that Great Lakes coho and chinook deteriorate rapidly when entering Great Lakes tributaries. The "toolie" strain of chinook (used exclusively in the Great Lakes) deteriorates almost as rapidly as chum salmon. The cohos darken up very quickly, often turning black within a few days. If the angler wants to tangle with fresh salmon that not only give a good fight but are also edible, he is going to have to know where to be and when.

The Upstream Journey

The initiation and progression of the salmon's upstream migration is to a large degree determined by water temperature. Spring chinook will not move when the water is below 50°. This is observed at dam sites. A heavy spring rain and/or cold spell will stop all traffic if the water drops below 50°. Springers like the water in the low fifties but will move freely up until the mid-sixties. Beyond this point, they become lethargic, holding deep and taking little interest in anything. As the spring and summer progress, the water continues to warm. One might wonder how these fish could proceed to their fall spawning grounds if they won't move in warm water. The answer lies in the fact that the further they push into the headwaters, the colder the water gets. Therefore, conditions are such that they can continually move. It also must be said that our West Coast inland snowmelt streams, where the largest concentrations of springers are found, stay cool in their upper stretches. This is where the salmon have progressed to by mid-summer. Many of the Pacific coastal streams are too warm to support springers. This, in part, is due to natural circumstances. But, it is also a result of water diversion. One of the greatest enemies of the springer is water diversion. Springers need the cold water to survive. If too much water is diverted, the stream flow slows and the water warms to beyond the springer's range. This is sure death for this marvelous fish. Smolts migrating to sea won't survive in such warm water either. Sixty-five-degree water gives way to diseases that cause most of these smolts to perish.

With fall chinook and coho, we have a situation in reverse. The water temperature has to come down to at least the low to mid-50s for the salmon to move. However, these fish, like their spring cousins, also prefer the temperature to be in the low-50s. Thus, when fall chinook are holding in tidewater, it is the cooler upstream waters that are largely responsible for triggering them to move up the river.

Water level also has something to do with migration. Every year, I like to take a few trips down Oregon's Siuslaw River in September. The water temperature is generally in the mid-50s. I see a few stragglers around but never do I witness great migrations of salmon at this time. This was at first puzzling because I knew that once in the river, the salmon would move freely in such temperatures. While the mid-50 temperatures are adequate, the low flow is apparently not strong enough to trigger mass migrations up from tidewater. Here is where *volume* of water is needed. Once that first heavy fall rain comes, all hell breaks loose and the salmon fill the river. Apparently the salmon are more choosy in tidewater. Temperature and volume are both important.

There may also be a safety factor here. The chinooks are shy fish. They are often found in slow deep holes when the stream becomes low and clear. This may account for their complacency during early September.

You might ask, "What good is it to be concerned with water temperature if I live 60 miles from the salmon streams? I can't measure the water temperature from this distance. How could I obtain this information?" This is true but during the peak of the salmon migration, you can take note of all conditions that lead up to the peak of the run, such that you may be able to predict future runs with the same accuracy. How much rain fell? What was the air temperature when the rain fell? What direction was the wind coming from? How high did the river level rise? Certainly no two years are exactly alike but similar circumstances will help you to predict when and when not to take a salmon day, or a three-day fall salmon trip.

The locals who fish salmon in Michigan have a big advantage in this regard. I remember fishing Harrisville Harbor for salmon on Lake Huron. During one year in the mid-seventies, I spent a few days at the Harbor casting spinners for big chinook. Every angler I encountered during my first few days was from somewhere other than Harrisville. Finally, the weather shifted overnight and on my last day the locals showed up. The temperature had dropped due to a cold northeasterly wind which they say blew the fish into the Harbor where they were accessible to anglers. Apparently they were right. We all caught more salmon in the first four hours of sunlight than we had caught in three full days of fishing. This is when I began to realize how important timing was when in pursuit of salmon.

This large buck was taken on a Winter Steelhead Standard in low water. Jed Davis photo

Holding Water

Where salmon hold in rivers is perhaps one of the most misunderstood aspects of technique. It's not that anglers fish water where salmon never hold as much as it is neglecting different types of water where salmon do hold. As spinner fishermen, we have limitations. When salmon hold in fast/deep runs of large West Coast inland snowmelt rivers, it is nearly impossible to get our lure to the bottom. The water is simply too swift and too deep to run even a lead-bodied No. 5 spinner to the bottom. Besides, it isn't much fun even to try. One reaction to this situation is to fish other methods. A better alternative is to seek waters that are suited to spinner fishing.

Coho and chinook seek seven basic types of waters: fast/deep runs, fast/deep tailouts, the edge of a deep run and boiling water, slack water pools, deep riffled pools, head of a drift (below the chutes), and spawning riffles. The fast/deep runs of 15 to 25 feet are very difficult to spinner fish. When such waters are encountered as on the Cowlitz, Middle Fork Willamette, I find that it is better to use lead and a drifter or to back-troll from a boat. As explained above, it becomes a chore just to get the spinner on the bottom. Even if successful, as soon as resistance is put on the lure, it rapidly surfaces out of the salmon's range. Better to fish this water with other methods.

Salmon do hold in tailouts but they are somewhat more picky than steelhead. Whereas a steelhead will expose itself in ten inches of clear water, salmon like tailouts to be somewhat protected in one or a combination of several ways. Protection is provided by water speed, depth, off-colored water, or broken surface. These waters are often an extension of the fast/deep runs discussed above, the difference being that they are shallower and thus more easily negotiated with a spinner. These are good waters to seek out for spring chinook because salmon holding here will be moving or will have recently moved. A salmon will always be more aggressive in new holding water. This makes tailouts good candidates for springer spinner fishing. This, however, is not true for fall chinook. Fall chinook that lie in tailouts are generally old and dark fish that have reached their upstream destination and are on the verge of spawning. Such fish are worthless table fare and provide poor sport.

Salmon holding below a natural upstream barrier can often be found to hold right at the edge of slack boiling water and a fast run. This water is very difficult to spinner fish due to the influence of many currents at one time in a small area. Drifters bounce their lead and eggs at the edge of the current. I have had luck jigging spinners off the bottom. One man is at the oars guiding the boat down the entire edge of the confluence of the two currents. The other man jigs his spinner off the bottom in three-foot pulls. It is important not to jerk the spinner off the bottom but rather pull in a steady methodical motion. The salmon will follow the lure and strike on the upward pull. Try it. It can be very effective!

Slack water salmon can be very difficult although it must be said that coho are easier than chinook. One often sees these fish porpoising or jumping in a slack pool or under a large overhanging oak tree close to shore. Although active and seemingly aggressive, these fish are, in reality, quite timid, showing very little interest in spinners except at dawn, dusk, or during a favorable weather change. They otherwise seem most negotiable with bait drifted from a bobber. I spend very little time with these fish. In most cases, these salmon have progressed as far upriver as they will go. They hold in slack water, adjacent to where they plan to spawn, just waiting for their eggs to ripen. They jump in an effort to shake loose egg skeins. One notices that these salmon are for the most park dark and beyond any food value. In my early years, I used to spend considerable time chasing these salmon. I now totally ignore them.

Deep-riffled pools of a modest speed are salmon meccas often ignored by salmon enthusiasts. I must tell a story in this regard that ironically occurred two days ago. Hayden Bridge is a boat launch on the lower McKenzie River. This is a very popular shore and boat spot for three reasons. First, a natural chute above the bridge causes fish to congregate in this spot. Second, the bridge itself provides cover. Third, a warm-water discharge attracts spring chinook and summer steelhead when the water in the McKenzie is in the 40s and low 50s. Everyone who fishes this site congregates at the warm-water dischcharge or below the chute. A bit further downstream lies a riffled pool that has a chop to it and is about five feet deep. No one fishes it. I arrived at Hayden Bridge at 9:30 a.m. About ten anglers had worked the discharges and chute area real hard from 4:30 a.m. on with not one fish. After a nice chat with a shore angler, I launched my boat and headed for the pool which, as usual, hadn't been touched all morning. I started to cover the pool when on the tenth cast, a 15-pound springer struck.

Riffled pools as described above form from gravel or small rock tailouts that have a gradually descending slope. In other words, instead of a white water chute at the break, the bottom contour gradually deepens into a pool. Salmon (and steelhead) love this water because they can seek a depth at which they feel most comfortable with but at the same time enjoy the protection of the riffled surface. In addition, the water is not so fast as to tax much of their energy. Best of all, this is perfect spinner water. These pools never seem to be deeper than ten feet which means that even a No. 3 spinner can be worked quite nicely. I take more salmon, especially springers, from this water than any other type of water.

Fishing salmon directly below chutes is very much akin to classic steelheading. The fish hold in a run directly below the head of the pool. Salmon are more prone to hold in this water when the temperature is in the mid- to upper-fifties and above, in the smaller rivers, and when fish are on the move. These conditions generally describe fall salmon fishing which is when I have my best luck in this type of water.

Just about anyone who has ever fished for salmon has observed spawning fish in shallow gravel bars. These fish should be left alone! They are of little food value, have very little fight left, and are so easy to catch that little challenge is offered in pursuit of them. What's more, if these fish are left to successfully spawn, they will provide a continued healthy run of fish in years to come. Like the sign says, "Kill your fish, kill your fishing . . . dead fish don't spawn."

It is important to note here that while we have discussed salmon holding water, the emphasis has been on the uniqueness of salmon water in relation to steelhead. For example, salmon hold in slack water and boiling water where steelhead don't. In the final analysis, there are more similarities than dissimilarities as to where salmon and steelhead hold. If you have steelhead experience, this should be your basic starting point with salmon. We must, however, distinguish between summer and winter steelhead. Aside from the deep riffled pools described above, summer-runs and salmon (typically springers) don't mix. It is the winter not summer steelhead holding water that has the most in common with salmon holding water.

One additional point needs to be made about salmon holding water. I know that I have mentioned it again and againt but you can't underestimate the importance of remaining flexible in the type of water you approach and how you approach it. I have had countless salmon days in which I picked up my only fish in an odd place. When you fish a new drift for salmon, don't assume you know it until you have fished it several times. Salmon are much less predictable than steelhead. Say "no" or "never" to where a salmon will hold and the next fish will make you eat your words. Exceptions are the rule in salmon fishing.

Environmental Factors

All the factors discussed in Chapters 6 and 7 apply pretty much to salmon as they do to steelhead. Two factors have always stood out in my fishing experience that seem to influence salmon fishing the most. These are *weather changes* and *direct sunlight.*

Salmon, chinook in particular, react very favorably during a weather change. During a transition, the fish begin to move around. They become more active and are thus more likely to hit. The shift in conditions may be toward an unfavorable set of circumstances but, just before and during the transition, the fish seem to hit well. For example, if I am fishing under morning clouds, I typically get a fish just before the sun comes out at 11:00 a.m. Being on the river at dawn or at dusk also has a similar consequence.

The problem with this knowledge is that it doesn't do us much good in the respect that we can't control weather changes or predict exactly when a weather change takes place. After all, I'm talking about transition periods of 15 or 20 minutes. What we can do is be on the river at dawn or dusk. This helps. We can also pick more favorable days if this coincides with when the salmon are running. For example, let's say the water has just come up and I know the fishing will be good for the next two or three days. On Tuesday, it will be cloudy all day; on Thursday, intermittent showers; on Friday, sunny all day. I will fish Thursday. The intermittent showers will produce constantly changing conditions. This means that there may be many transition periods during the day in which salmon will become activated.

The second factor that heavily influences salmon fishing is direct sunlight. Chinook, especially chinook, react very unfavorably to direct sunlight when the water temperature is above 50°. This doesn't mean they are uncatchable. It does mean that they lie low and are difficult to get to strike, especially in streams that are running clear. In off-colored streams, those that have a green, gray, or roily-brown cast, the fish are less affected. My experience with salmon and sunlight has taught me to carefully pick my salmon days. If I fish a sunny day, those fish better be fresh and on the move and the water better be on the high side, off-colored and cold. If I decide to go, I'll be on the water at first light to take full advantage of the dawn. If conditions are any less than the latter, I'll wait for a cloudy/rainy day. Fishing for chinooks in low water and in direct sunlight can often be an act in futility. If, however, you find yourself on a salmon stream with a gleaming sun shining its way onto the water's surface, look for a good chute where the head of the pool has a highly broken surface. Use a small dull-finished spinner in size 1 or 2. If you can't get to the bottom, attach a split-shot 15 inches above your spinner. This setup worked a number of times for me.

Being There

At various intervals in this book, I have made a big play for understanding the environment, salmonid behavior, and knowing how to approach your fish. I'm all for the right rods, reels and lures but when it comes to fishing salmon, nothing is more important than knowing when and where not to be on the river. Give me rusty spinners, rotten eggs and temperamental plugs and if I am on the river during the most optimal time, I will outfish the guy who has the best of everything but no sense of timing.

Planning salmon trips a month in advance is likely to lead to disappointment. No one can ever predict when that first fall rain that brings the salmon up will come. For example, in my first three autumns in Oregon, the peak of the chinook run on my rivers has fluctuated greatly. In 1981, it wasn't hot until November 10th; in '82, October 25th; and in '83, October 15th. If you want to get in on some good action when the fish are fresh and most eager, you need to consider the environment. And why is timing so important for salmon? Except for spring chinook which mature slowly, fall salmon relative to steelhead move up a stream quickly, mature quickly and are spawning in a matter of a few days or a week. Whereas a steelhead or springer may stay bright for a month or more, fall salmon (especially coho

A fish plays the author on the North Branch of the Pentwater, a Michigan stream. Asa Pearl photo

or a toolie strain chinook salmon) lose their desirability over a very short time. This doesn't leave us much time to go after them. We want to intercept them when they are fresh from the estuary or ocean. The best predictors for this are 1) cooler nighttime temperatures which cool the water and 2) those first big fall rains. On the West Coast, it is easy to predict when this happens for fall salmon. Follow the river stage levels all summer and you will see that from July on, the river level stays fairly constant. If an early fall rain raises the level by one inch, I don't jump. But when that first heavy rain pushes the river level up by three to six inches, I know

that those salmon will be moving in. In the Great Lakes states where no river level information is available, you have to learn how much rainfall is needed to raise the river to a sufficient level such that the salmon come in. For example, .33 or more inches was enough to bring the salmon up one of my Michigan rivers. I would call the weather station in that particular area and find out how much rain had fallen. I also could easily obtain air temperature readings for the area so, within a few years, I could predict, with some degree of accuracy, what water temperatures corresponded to a certain air temperature. Mind you, the relationship between these two factors is not always the same. As I pointed out in an earlier steelhead chapter, a given air temperature does not always correspond to a given water temperature but, in the case of salmon, at least I could obtain some rough idea of what was happening and then make an educated guess as to whether I should drive 180 miles to my river.

Spinner Technique

In the steelhead chapters, I discussed that it was important to try to maintain a slow blade-spin when fishing the spinner for steelhead. As it is important for steelhead, it is even more important when pursuing salmon. This realization hit home when fishing for Michigan salmon in the early years of the Great Lakes salmon program. Thousands upon thousands of fish would ascend the Platte River. Many of these would hold in Loon Lake for a time before moving further up the Platte. Anglers would line up where the Platte dumps into Loon Lake and try for coho. Everyone caught fish but it always seemed that two or three anglers always did the best. Like most everyone, I was new to the sport so I watched the successful anglers very closely. I remember being very frustrated one year. My boat was right next to another boat. We were using the same spinners and casting into the same places but they were getting the fish. I finally realized that it was the slow blade-spin that was doing the trick.

Coho and chinook each have a unique trait that makes fishing the spinner slowly imperative. Coho are followers. They will sometimes follow a spinner and strike as it is being lifted out of the water. Therefore, it is very important that when your spinner has swung around and is directly below the boat that you reel slowly at least halfway to the boat. They will often follow a long time before striking.

Chinook have their own peculiarity. They always hesitate before striking. They follow the spinner and just at the point you think they will strike, they hesitate as if examining the lure. In order to accommodate this hesitation, a slow retrieval insures that they will have the opportunity to examine and then strike.

Salmon Spinners

Good salmon spinners possess all the desirable qualities of winter steelhead spinners. Most importantly, they should be weighted for depth. Although cohos will move great distances to take a spinner, chinook generally won't. Furthermore, chinook are strictly bottom fish. This means that drifting your spinner to get down to the bottom and keeping it there will be a top priority. Thus, for effective fishing you need a heavily weighted lure. The placement of translucent red beads on the shaft is a no-no. They do nothing for the spinner and take up valuable room that can be used for weighting with lead or solid brass. Bear Valleys, Tee-Spoons, and Flash 'N Glos may be adequate spinners for tidewater trolling but for river fishing, they will put you at a severe disadvantage. You have to be able to cut through currents and go deep. On very small streams or Great Lakes tributaries with a gentle current, weighting is less of a concern but if you plan to fish a typical Northwest or Alaskan stream, you definitely need the weighting.

Coho and chinook salmon are a bit less picky about colored adornments than are steelhead. Reds, yellows, oranges, greens and blues will all take salmon in all seasons. However, there are certain colors that seem to provide some advantage under some conditions. Yellows and greens are very effective in water over 50°. Reds and oranges are excellent choices when fishing in water below 50°. When it comes to spring chinook, I am a *green* fanatic. The combination of fluorescent kelly green on brass has been dynamite. In the fall, yellows and chartreuse are excellent for fall chinook. When the cohos come in, the water temperature drops to 50° and below so my spinners vary between yellows and fluorescent red/oranges. If you find yourself on a stream that is low and clear, black-bladed spinners and plain tarnished brass spinners are a good choice for spooky fish.

Blade finish is also a concern but, as with colored adornments, salmon are less picky than steelhead in that they will be almost equally responsive to a variety of blades. Silver is desirable in water below 48° or 50° as its added flash turns on stubborn low-metabolismed fish. In warmer flows, I have not noticed any significant advantage to silver, brass, or copper. The exception might come with black blades. At times, salmon are very responsive to small spinners with a black oxide blade. However, the responsiveness is usually found with darkening pre-spawning salmon—fish that are less desirable in terms of fighting ability and food value. One blade finish that some salmon anglers swear by is a blade that is half silver, half gold (genuine silver and gold!). The finishes are divided vertically on the blade, not horizontally. This blade was typically found on the "C. P. Swing." It is also available on certain lures such as the Williams "Whitefish." I have worked with silver/gold blades. They are good for all trout and salmon but the cost of a blade composed of genuine gold and silver is so high that few have ever been commercially offered.

Anglers who use these silver/gold blades swear by them. Why would a combination finish be so effective? I have put a lot of thought and experimentation into this question. Genuine gold and silver plate are the brightest, flashiest plates you can buy. Yes, there is also rhodium and platinum, both of which are brighter but would you pay $5.00 for a blade? Wire line lake trout (mackinaw) trollers in Canada have found that a silver-plated Williams "Whitefish" works but under cloud cover, whereas the gold-plated model works best under sunny conditions. There is even a gold/silver model that is used in partly cloudy conditions or at dawn/dusk on a sunny day. The few of us who fish gold-plated winter steelhead spinners have found that gold works best on sunny days and in off-colored water. The silver plate is better in off-colored and/or cloudy conditions. By using a gold/silver combination, you are covered for all conditions and the result is one very versatile lure.

A few words on spinner size. A lot of anglers feel that if they are fishing for large salmon, they have to use a large spinner. Such beliefs have no basis. Many of my biggest salmon have come on a tiny spinner while fishing for trout. What's more important than size is getting the spinner to where the fish are . . . on the bottom. If you are fishing a prime five-foot pool in which you can reach the bottom with a No. 2 or 3 spinner, these sizes are often equally as effective as the larger spinners. If the sun is out or the fish are spooky, the smaller spinners will yield far better results than the larger spinners.

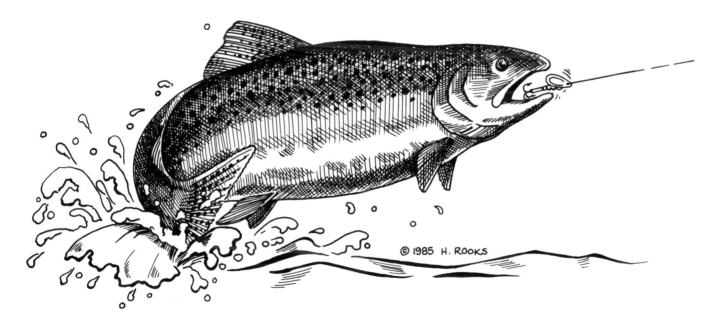

© 1985 H. ROOKS

Chapter 14

Spinners for Steelhead, Salmon and Trout

IN THIS FINAL CHAPTER, WE WILL TAKE A look at some of the homemade spinners commonly used for steelhead, salmon and trout throughout North America. By no means do I claim this presentation to be complete. Being the first book of its kind devoted solely to this topic, there was very little in the way of references to be used other than those I came across in magazines or by personal correspondence or contact. To a large extent, these spinners represent my personal repertoire of spinners. However, credit is given to those individuals who either inspired or popularized each of the lures.

Releasing a coho into the South Umpqua. David Davis photo

Each of the spinners presented is a proven fish-getter for the fish it is recommended for. Should you be skilled not only at reading water but also at fishing the spinner, I can confidently state that you will do well with these lures. (But, remember, I have not nor will I ever fish all steelhead and salmon rivers. Certain colors or finishes may be better suited to your area. Be flexible!) If, however, you are new to this type of angling, a spinner will only be as good as the skill you have to match it with. Spinners don't catch fish . . . fishermen do!

As you scrutinize the color plates and the corresponding discussion, keep one important thing in mind. Every piece of metal, tape and tubing placed on a spinner I use has a specific purpose. The same holds true for the order of placement of parts on the spinner shaft. I don't place a piece of fluorescent tape on a blade because it looks good to me. I don't order brass beads on the spinner shaft because they look right. I think solely in terms of getting to the fish and exciting them into striking. If a part or order or arrangement does not serve that purpose, it is of no use to me. If you are used to going into a tackle shop and seeing glittering spinners and macho/sexy packaging, you may be somewhat startled at the simplicity of the spinners presented. Commercially-designed spinners are designed to catch fishermen. We are not under the same criteria here. We need only to deal with what works.

All spinners presented here, regardless of finish or color, etc., are standardized within a given size. That is, I would always build a No. 3 in the exact same way. In this regard, I am striving to achieve two goals, each very important:

1) maximum weighting, 2) a responsive blade that spins on command and at very slow speeds. As I pointed out in Chapter 3, a spinner weighted beyond a certain point will start to decrease the responsiveness of the blade. Therefore,

each of these spinners has been designed such that the *maximum amount of weight* is used without decreasing blade responsiveness. Should you decide to go heavier, you will sacrifice blade responsiveness for weight. However, should you desire a lighter spinner, you have an almost limitless array of possibilities. With regard to the latter, this may be desirable for Great Lakes fishing where streams are shallow and of a more gentle flow when compared to the Pacific Northwest. Living in Oregon, I have had to deal with fast streams and their deep pools. Therefore, my orientation leans toward maximum weighting.

Below is a chart of my recommendations for spinner construction in sizes 0 through 5 using .032-in. French-type blades. Should you wish to build any spinner down on the color plate, just follow the chart and you are all set. All parts are available from firms listed in Chapter 3. Another noteworthy comment: Spinners are traditionally displayed with the outside of the blade (raised dome) resting against the body. Because throughout this book I have strongly recommended placing colored adornments on the *inside* of the blade and *not* the outside, I displayed a sample on the color plate to show how it is done.

The result is the flashiest, most colorful lure known to the spinner fisherman. Because of its reflectivity, steelhead and salmon can be excited from great distances of ten to 15 feet. Its ability to excite will cause otherwise low-metabolised steelhead to chase it 20 feet or right to the boat. In the most commonly used No. 5 size, it is balanced to perfection with instantaneous responsiveness. Sizes 2, 3 and 4 can also be used under varying conditions. I like to use No. 3s in low water/shallow conditions.

The major credit for this spinner must be given to the Michigan steelheaders and my efforts to promote it on the west coast. Written about extensively in many of the Great Lakes magazines, this is one lure that is used by some of the finest steelhead spinner fishermen in North America. Experienced anglers will always tell you how they get steelhead to chase their spinner in 32 degree water during a typically cold midwest winter.

I have personally found this silver/fire-orange combination to be most effective in water 52° and below. What this typically means for Northwest angling is that it starts to become effective in late November and stays effective right

Construction of Spinners Displayed on Color Plates

Spinner	Hook[a]	Shaft[b]	Body[c]	Blade[d]	Clevis[e]	Swivel[f]
No. 0	No. 6, 7, or 8	.030-in. wire	Dynamic SLO	0	No. 1	--
No. 1	No. 6 or 7	.030-in. wire	Dynamic SL1	1	No. 1	--
No. 2	No. 5 or 6	.030-in. wire	Dynamic SL1 or SL3	2	No. 2	--
No. 3	No. 2, 3 or 4[g]	.030-in. wire	Dynamic SL, SX or SS3 depending on depth or speed	3	No. 2	No. 12 Romer or Rosco black barrel
No. 4	No. 2, 3 or 4[g]	.030-in. wire	Dynamic SL, SX or SS4 depending on depth or speed	4	No. 2	No. 12 Romer or Rosco black barrel
No. 5	No. 2	.030-in. wire	Dynamic SL, SX or SS5 depending on depth or speed	5	No. 2	No. 12 Romer or Rosco black barrel

[a]VMC 9649B or Mustad 35647 round bend tables are recommended.

[b]3-in. shaft with preformed eye recommended.

[c]Solid one-piece brass beads are offered by Pen Tac. Brass balls may be substituted from other manufacturers. If going this route, reverse last two beads to center-balance spinner.

[d]Blades shown on color plate from Pen Tac. Similar blades are available from the other mail-order houses listed on page 26. On size #3 and up .032" brass is preferred with .0247" being the minimally acceptable thickness. Pen Tac 4 1/2 is equal to Worth/Lakeland #5 supplied by other mail-order houses.

[e]All suppliers use the same numbering system on clevises so don't worry about getting the right ones.

[f]Clevis sizes correspond to Worth's numbering system of "easy spin" clevis. This is a stirrup clevis. No. 1 of the same.

[g]No. 4 most commonly used for steelhead and trout, No. 2 or 3 for large salmon.

Winter Steelhead Standard

For most winter steelhead conditions, this is, without a doubt, one of the finest spinners that can be used. The tool of a professional, it has certain qualities that are unmatched by any mass-produced spinner. Both the body and blade are genuine silver-plated. Flourescent fire-orange tape is placed on the inside of the blade with tubing to match.

through the season. The smaller No. 2s, 3s, and 4s will take summer steelhead and trout under cloudy conditions throughout the season but, in my opinion, the red is not as effective as the yellow or green. If, however, you find yourself on an early summer steelhead stream with temperatures in the high 40s, the red will be very effective. Remember, water temperature, not time nor strain, determines effectiveness. Also, remember, this is an excellent salmon lure!

Green Standard

The exact same lure as above except for the color of the tape and shank tubing. Excellent for summer steelhead under cloudy conditions. Also excellent for spring Chinook and coho under the same conditions. With time, this color combination is gaining more and more favor with anglers at all times of year. On Oregon's Deschutes and Alsea, this combination in a #4 or #5 respectively has been tops.

Chartreuse Standard

Chartreuse tape and tubing on silver in cold-water conditions is right up there with fire orange. If you go through with red and think a fish should have been there, go through with chartreuse. Chartreuse will also have slightly more visibility in off-colored water.

This 13-lb. Alaska rainbow was taken at the confluence of Lake Iliamna and the Krichak rivers with a winter steelhead standard. Jed Davis photo

Asa Pearl's Special

I named this spinner after Asa Pearl, a close friend and one of the finest steelhead spinner fishermen I have ever seen. Although now living in Washington, D. C., he spent many years working in Michigan while enjoying some fine angling also. Somewhat annoyed by claims that steelhead under heavy pressure from anglers can only be taken with two- and four-pound-test line, he continually startled Michigan lite-liners (noodle rod anglers) by taking fish from under their noses with ten-pound line and small spinners. When asked to comment on his success, he would only say, "There is more to presentation than long leaders, light lines and tiny baits."

Asa Pearl's Special was first tried when he came out to fish with me in Oregon. Wanting to get away from it all, he insisted we be on a remote stream away from crowds. This was an opportunity for me to work on an angling problem that I was encountering. I was fishing some very small streams that were fast and which held steelhead in deep pockets. I needed a heavy spinner to cut the water but, under sunny conditions, my silver-plated 5s were spooking the steelhead. My solution was to use a very toned-down No. 5. Blade and body were brass. Black chenille (used by fly tiers) was wrapped around the hook shank and black tape was used on the inside of the blade. In addition, I placed a solitary fluorescent red dot in the middle of the black tape for just a touch of bright attraction. The dots were cut using an Osborne No. 155 Revolving Punch.

We arrived at the river under beautiful sunny skies that shone brightly on the water's surface. The river was on the low side. It was a perfect setting to try the new spinner. We took seven steelhead. I named the spinner after my good friend.

Columbia Gorge

This pattern was invented by some customers. I received a call one day in early September. The angler made a sizable order and said he had hooked 20 steelhead below McNary Dam on the Columbia. In the next week, half our business came from the tri-cities area (Richland, Pasco and Kennewick) in Washington. So I knew he hooked *at least five steelhead.*

This is a very simple pattern used on the Columbia and Deschutes in sizes 4, 4 1/2, and 5. It employs a black oxide body and either a brass, electric brass or 24K gold blade. A 24K gold blade is used on color plate. This is a big water spinner that seems most effective when the water has stain to it or the water is just plain dirty. It has really proven itself in the summer in the Columbia Gorge!

Black & Black

A lot of anglers will not fish high muddy water. This spinner could be your ticket if you know where to find your fish in these conditions. I watched a friend hook 5 steelhead on this spinner in one hole and then I, too, became a believer. The spinner is simple. Black oxide blade and black oxide body with the hook of your choice, either single or treble.

Why black? Wouldn't silver be the ticket under low visibility conditions. No! The two most effective colors under these conditions are 24K gold and black. This is what the fish can see best. And I might add that this is not only true for salmon and steelhead. It is also true for resident trout, smallmouth bass and just about any species.

Summer Green

This is a summer steelhead spinner I developed on the McKenzie, South Santiam and North Umpqua rivers. This rare fluorescent Kelly green tape comes from Pen Tac and the matching tubing is also from Pen Tac. This is a fantastic lure for cloudy conditions when temperatures are 50° to 57°. Although I have tried, this spinner is hard to beat. I have not yet found one that can beat it for the conditions for which it is designed.

The spinner is used in No. 3 size 95 percent of the time. You can use a No. 4 but the No. 3 is so well-weighted and balanced that there is no reason to go to a No. 4 that may spook summer-runs under various conditions. Brass or gold plate is the way to go. Silver can be good in temperatures 48° to 51°. If you fish summer steelhead, try it. Also excellent for trout and spring chinook. This one is a real winner!

McKenzie Medium

This is a spinner developed for taking summer-runs in bright sunlight and in clear water. In an effort to tone the lure down as much as possible, the blade and brass beads are purposely tarnished. A piece of dark green (or black) prism tape is applied to the blade and the hook shank is left blank. The result is a spinner that gives "presence" without spooking steelhead. It is best fished within a foot of the surface and will produce thunderous strikes when zigzagged or waked (see "Surface Presentations," Chapter 8) in shallow riffles. This spinner is an answer to "expert" drift fishermen and lure fishermen who think you have to be on the river at 4:00 a.m. to be successful with summer-runs. I take 50 to 75 summer-runs per season. The majority of these are taken in bright sunlight in the middle of the day. Fish it in size 2 in riffles, size 1 in tailouts.

McKenzie Dark

Same as the McKenzie Medium but with a black blade (industrial "Black Oxide," see Chapter 4). This is my favorite spinner to use in sunny summer-run conditions. The lure gives the impression of a Mayfly Nymph or Caddis in the water. The black blade totally absorbs all light. Thus, fish are not threatened.

Although I am not aware of anyone who makes this lure for summer-run fishing, commercial models such as the *Panther Martin* are popular for fishing the Rogue's half-pounders. This is also a very versatile trout lure. I have taken many a beautiful red-side rainbow. Dynamite on cutthroat, and good for all other trout in temperatures above 52°.

Trout Standard

Used with silver-, brass-, or gold-finished blade and beads, this lure, in sizes 0, 1 and 2 is excellent for all trout in cloudy, shaded, or low-light conditions in temperatures above 52°. In temperatures below 52°, it is also good in sunny conditions. Fluorescent red tape is used on the blade with matching latex tubing on the hook shank. Many imitations of this exist in stores, but none comes close to matching the rich fluorescence of the red used. The lure is also weighted more heavily than most commercial models and yet spins on command. This allows one to cast from long distances to wary trout.

A McKenzie redside taken on a McKenzie Dark. These fish form the backbone of the McKenzie wild trout population and should be released. Jed Davis photo

Ed's Pregnant

Developed by my good friend Ed Davis, Rogue River guide, this spinner was named after a pot belly that has always made this salmon/steelhead genius look pregnant. Not much you can say about this one. It employs a silver blade with black tape on inside and a black oxide body. This is a fabulous lure. Use in any size for any species in any location of the United States in just about any set of conditions. A proven winner! Trout, steelhead, salmon, char. You name it.

Black Mallard

Another special-purpose spinner designed for steelhead, salmon, and trout that are holding in deep waters but are nonetheless spooky due to warm water, angling pressure, or any adverse condition. The spinner employs a black oxide blade and black oxide beads. Kelly green, chartreuse, or red dots are placed on the inside of the blade in a symmetrical pattern. A small piece of matching tubing is placed behind the last bead. Use as large a size as is needed to get to the bottom. Fish very slowly. My experience is that fish will hit very hard. A variation employs brass beads if more visibility is desired.

Perspective 1993

Although *Spinner Fishing for Steelhead, Salmon and Trout* is in its third edition, changes in technique and spinner selection have not changed that much in the past ten years. I wrote the initial edition of this book between 1982 and 1984. At that time, eggs and plugs (and some flies in the summer) were about the only thing you saw on the river. Spinners have now earned their rightful place although this technique is still practiced by far fewer anglers than the other more established methods. When it comes to die-hard steelheaders, tradition is very difficult to change.

Because spinner fishing occupies a unique niche in terms of its ability to cover **all** types of water more quickly, as compared to other methods, I feel there is still a lot of opportunity to zero in on a niche that is being untapped. This view is supported by customers that patronize our spinner component division. A guy from Ohio will hook several fish among a group of egg fishermen. An angler on Idaho's Snake will clobber the steelhead when the plug-pulling guides will go fishless. This isn't to suggest that spinners always outfish eggs or plugs. In reality, there are probably many times when the latter two methods outdo spinners. What it is saying is this: There is a niche for this method which is still largely untapped.

In looking to the third edition of this book, I had an important decision to make. Should I completely redo the book or should I just make the necessary changes where absolutely needed? I decided on the latter because I didn't want to change the character and feel of the book. It was written at a very happy time in my life and in some ways, the text and photos are a reminder or a documentation of that time. I just didn't want to disturb it. So I have largely left it unchanged from the first edition. However, there are a few worthwhile notes that I would like to add here:

1) 24K gold blades are now available. They are expensive and if you choose to purchase them, they should have a deep rich yellow/orange color. If they are very faded or are close to silver in looks, they are no good. Gold is to brass as silver is to nickel. Brass, especially electric brass, is a great finish but genuine 24K gold is even better...if you want to spend the extra money.

2) When buying Kelly green tape, make sure that the exact color of the tape matches the tubing. This color is rare and 3M stopped making it in the mid 1980s. A lot of people will tell you they have Kelly green but the acid test is matching tape color to tubing. The tubing is easy to find so this should be your guide.

3) On the color plate, you will see a broad French blade and a narrow one. The narrow blades have less water resistance and are used for steelhead and trout in fast shallow riffles. The reason the narrow blade is used is because it is much more stable in fast water (due to decreased water resistance) and we found that when fishing for summer steelhead under these conditions, the fish want a stable lure that guides through the water like a fly. That is what these narrow blades do. Pen Tac offers these under the "Dingbat" label. I am not aware of any other manufacturer that has these although this does not mean they do not exist.

4) A very good combination to try when you want maximum visibility is a silver/24K gold blade. The reason this combination works so well is that silver and gold reflect different types of light. Therefore, you hit two birds with one stone by reflecting two different colors on the same lure.

5) Fluorescent blue tape and tubing has come on in a big way in the past two years. Used with 24K gold or silver, many anglers now really depend on it. Give it a try.

Index